LITURGY

With Style and Grace

LITURGY

With Style and Grace

Gabe Huck

Gerald T. Chinchar

LTP

LITURGY
TRAINING
PUBLICATIONS

acknowledgments

Texts quoted in this book are acknowledged under "Sources," beginning on page 131.

LITURGY WITH STYLE AND GRACE © 1998, Archdiocese of Chicago: Liturgy Training Publications, 1800 North Hermitage Avenue, Chicago IL 60622-1101; 1-800-933-1800; orders@ltp.org; fax 1-800-933-7094. All rights reserved. Visit our website at www.ltp.org.

This book was edited by Martin Connell. Audrey Novak Riley and Bryan Cones were the production editors. The design is by Kristyn Kalnes, and the typesetting was done by Jim Mellody-Pizzato in Sabon and Baker Signet. This book was printed by Von Hoffmann Graphics, Inc. of Eldridge, Iowa.

Library of Congress Catalog Card Number 98-86330

04 03 02 01 00   6 5 4 3 2

ISBN 1-56854-186-4

LSG3

Each church gathers regularly

to praise and thank God,

to remember and make present God's great deeds,

to offer common prayer,

to realize and celebrate the kingdom of peace and justice.

That action of the Christian assembly is liturgy.

Environment and Art in Catholic Worship

Contents

Before We Begin

he name *Liturgy with Style and Grace* gives rise to an incarnational vision of liturgy. This book explores some of the ways that human beings use their various talents to acknowledge God's gracious presence and action in their midst. Implied thoughout this book is the conviction that in these human gestures, God graces us. As Christian people we are convinced that the paschal mystery of Jesus has definitively and positively altered the course of human history. Our celebrations of the liturgy provide a way for us, God's holy and priestly people, to ask this saving reality to touch us and change us.

Over and over in this book we talk about the human actions that we do in the liturgy. These actions are not for the sake of drama or poetry alone, though these art forms are an important part of our full human identity. We use the best of ourselves as a way of intentionally inviting the grace of Jesus the Christ into our midst.

Thus, this is a book for members of parish liturgy committees and planning teams, for those who have a ministry at the liturgy—for anyone who wishes to learn more about the liturgy. It is for newcomers and for those who want a refresher course. It can be used by one person or by a group, and can be read and discussed at just about any pace that seems right.

In these pages we will study the liturgy as something that people do. To that extent, our approach is not from theology, or from history, or from church legislation. All of these are important—crucial—to a full understanding of liturgy. But before we can study our theology, before we can make sense of our history, before we can work with our church legislation, we have to know clearly what we are talking about: We have to know liturgy as a certain form of human activity. When we keep a season like Advent, when we have a wedding, when we sing the Great Amen or come forward to receive communion, when we make the sign of the cross: In all these we are doing something that is part of a human form of expression for the individual and the community, a ritual. Ministers and planners with a sure sense of the ways we use ritual as human beings and as Christians have a solid background to their work.

What is presented here is an overview. It is to point out certain aspects of liturgy, and perhaps to stir up your desire to understand and appreciate the liturgy even more. The quality of our common prayer of liturgy is sometimes not as strong as it could be, not because we lack a theology or a spirituality, but because we sometimes do the human things without having thought deeply about them. We sometimes forget that liturgy is our common action. We leave the actions of liturgy off by itself somewhere for professionals and scholars to think about, a domain we visit every Sunday but perhaps are never fully at home in. Perhaps this book is simply to help us all feel more at home with liturgy.

You will not find complete programs or detailed analyses in this book. Instead, it offers a context in which to view practical issues. A group using this book may find common understandings, a common vocabulary—tools for their work in liturgy. Sometimes, those working with liturgy are so busy with details that they have not been able to take an opportunity to form a clear vision of the whole. The approach of this book is to offer planners and ministers a way to share a sense of all the ways liturgy expresses the life of a parish.

The articles have been grouped in six units, followed by the bibliography and sources.

- *First Things.* Some basic thoughts are presented here on liturgy and Christian life.
- *The Elements of Liturgy.* We pray together with words, sounds, gestures, places and objects. This unit is about each of these and how they come together.
- *Who Does the Liturgy?* Here are articles on the assembly and the various ministries: presider, lectors, ushers and more.
- *The Mass.* The Mass is the rite that most of us experience most often. It has its own unit so that we can consider its parts in detail.
- *Days and Seasons.* Prayer has its rhythms through days and years. This unit is an introduction to the seasons.
- *The Rites of the Church.* Here are considerations of the liturgies that mark initiation, marriage, sickness and other occasions.
- *Resources.* A bibliography is provided to demonstrate that there is lots to learn about the liturgy and as a handy guide for going further and deeper on any one topic.

With this new edition, some changes have been introduced. After each article, there are questions for further reflection and discussion. Moreover, the far right column now has quotations from a variety of sources to complement the issue. Some of these are from church documents; some from hymns, poetry and literature; a few are from scholars of the liturgy. The new elements are intended to encourage you to explore this particular aspect of the liturgy further and to invite examination of the way things are done in your community. This new edition has an extensive bibliography at the end for those who would like to do more reading on any particular topic discussed in this book.

When this book is used by a group, the leaders will want to draw from each article and unit additional questions for reflection and discussion besides those provided here. There should be ample time in the group's sessions for participants to bring up points in each unit that need elaboration or discussion. Participants should be encouraged to read each session's material with pencil in hand to underline, question and make marginal notes.

Whether you are reading this book alone or studying it with others, it is our hope that it will provoke thought, stimulate discussion and send you further into our liturgy and in knowing the gracious God who meets us there.

First Things

Before turning to any of the particular symbols of our worship, we consider the very nature of symbols as part of human life and as part of our religious heritage. Our symbols bring us together, wedding us not only to those who have gone before us marked with a sign of faith and those who have not yet lived, but knitting the members of our assemblies today to one another in faith. Our symbols carry the faith through time and place, ever leading us toward the source of life and grace.

What We Mean and Believe

he best of Jewish and Christian tradition tells those concerned with the way prayer happens to *beware*. Beware of forgetting that the prayers we make together are not religion. Beware of the tricky way appearances and realities have of getting mixed up. Beware of thinking that prayer is about rules or methods or special gifts or training.

This line of thought runs through the scriptures. In Isaiah's vision, the Lord says: "When you spread out your hands [in prayer], I close my eyes to you. Though you pray the more, I will not listen. Your hands are full of blood!" (Isaiah 1:15)

As anyone who works with the liturgy knows, the liturgy can become its own little world. We know, for example, that beautiful expression in music is a normal element of liturgy. Yet it is not beauty alone that makes liturgy. Likewise, if liturgy becomes solely a matter of laws and rubrics to be followed, it can be emptied of prayer, of its very self. Yet, being who we are, we need the laws and rubrics, the forms and traditions that have been handed on.

The scriptures and the deeds of our saints tell us that what is most delicate about liturgy is something beyond beauty and beyond law. People who do liturgy with strength are people whose lives need the rituals of the liturgy.

Now it is possible to make choices and do things that set up a perfectly reasonable, well-adjusted, perhaps even prosperous life that just doesn't need prayer. The person whose life is like that can put liturgy aside, or turn it into an art exhibit or a system for keeping God happy.

But a more human way is to fashion a life that needs prayer and needs ritual. The prayer is both our private conversation with the Lord and the repeated patterns that our tradition gives us. The ritual embraces these patterns of praying and includes also structured ways of keeping feasts and seasons, of fasting and of proclaiming scripture, of professing faith and renouncing evil.

Ritual and prayer are not meant to be present in our lives as obligation, as diversion, as education or as entertainment. They are not there as a magic way to salvation. Rather, they are there because we need them, because without them we could not be ourselves, could not be the church. Liturgy is the various rituals of the assembled church, the act of the assembled church. It is what we who are baptized need to do—the songs we need to sing, the words we need to hear, the gestures we need to make. *Need* because without them, we could not give our lives their gospel shape. In liturgy, we become what we need to be. The immersion in baptism's waters is the death we die to evil all our lives, is the new life we have in Christ. The bread broken and the cup poured out at the eucharist are the sacrifice and sharing we are to be for the world.

The experience of our people has been that a life of faithfulness to the Lord, of constant loving of God and neighbor and self, calls out for ritual expression, is sustained and nourished by ritual. We are sustained when the ritual is our deed, when in its beauty and simplicity it can carry and form us.

Ritual and life are not strangers to each other in our tradition. Rather, they create, nourish and sustain each other.

1. Who are your "saints" — whether they have been recognized by canonization in the church or not — whose examples have taught you the beauty, strength and transforming power of the liturgy? Think of ways in which your participation in the liturgy would follow their example.

2. When you find the rituals of the church merely something that you have to do, it's likely that something needs to change. Perhaps it's something in the ritual. Perhaps something in your life. Perhaps both. How can you become more involved in the rites of the church?

Each faithful individual is made aware of the unity which comprehends them on many and various occasions, but chiefly in the liturgy. In it they see themselves face to face with God, not as an entity, but as members of this unity. It is the unity which addresses God; the individual merely speaks in it, and it requires of the individual man or woman that they should know that they are a member of it.

It is on the plane of liturgical relations that the individual experiences the meaning of religious fellowship. The individual man and woman — provided that they actually desire to take part in the celebration of the liturgy — must realize that it is as members of the church that they, and the church within them, act and pray; they must know that in this higher unity they are at one with the rest of the faithful, and they must desire to be so.

Romano Guardini

The Christian hope of the future is that this, the true meaning and message of the incarnation, will come to be more deeply understood, and the demand on our worshiping love and total self-offering will receive a more complete response — stretching upward in awestruck contemplation to share that adoring vision of the Principle which is "the inheritance of the saints in light," and downwards and outwards in loving action, to embrace and so transform the whole world. When this happens, Christian sacramental worship will at last disclose its full meaning, and enter into its full heritage. For it will be recognized as the ritual sign of our deepest relation with Reality, and so of the mysterious splendour of our situation and our call: our successive life freely offered in oblation, and the abiding life of God in Christ received, not for our own sakes, but in order to achieve that transfiguration of the whole created universe, that shining forth of the splendour of the Holy, in which the aim of worship shall be fulfilled.

Evelyn Underhill

We Express in Symbols

he kind of prayer that parish liturgy planners and ministers are usually concerned with involves many people. It is the ritual of a community, of an assembly. The ritual of an assembly is not the same as ten or a hundred people each praying privately in the same space at the same time. Community ritual can happen on all sorts of occasions, from birthday parties to wakes to football games to wars. They are ways for people to express common attitudes and feelings and understandings that transcend mere words.

Consider weddings. Any society evolves ways to express what the union of a man and a woman means. These expressions can sometimes live longer than the meanings that they first conveyed (do you know what carrying the bride across the threshold meant to the people who first did it?). Generally, there are a whole series of activities—with words, songs, actions, objects—that convey beyond any philosophical or legal or religious or sociological language all that this society wants marriage to mean. In themselves, these things are simply elements from life—a ring, a kiss, a dance, hands joined together—but in the context of the society they have all kinds of meanings that express beyond any words what marriage is about. These ritual actions and objects can strengthen that meaning for the particular couples and for all who witness them.

Sometimes we are tempted to treat this matter of ritual as a kind of simple shorthand. During Advent, we sometimes hear that in the Advent wreath the circle means this and the candles mean that. Certainly there is value in telling the story behind the Advent wreath, and those meanings are indeed present. But the power of ritual can be diminished if we treat it as a way to teach a lesson, or as an equation where each element has its exact value. Ritual is far deeper. When it is done wholeheartedly and well, ritual touches many layers of ourselves at once.

It is barely right, for example, to say that the wedding ring, a circle, means that the union is to last forever, or that it is a sign that these two are bound together. It is really not the ring at all that is the symbol at work in this ritual: It is the giving of the ring, the putting on of the ring, the wearing of the ring. Who could tell the whole meaning of that in words? Rituals are never one-dimensional, never just an object or just a word. Within a community of people who share some vision of themselves and of what life is about, rituals have many dimensions. Rituals are always inseparable from the human beings doing the actions. Rituals are always ambiguous, defying us to classify or explain them.

So in the example of the Advent wreath, it is not what the candles can be said to stand for that makes it ritual, that is, that makes it belief embodied in symbol. Rather, what makes the wreath ritual is the doing of this special prayer: the reverent lighting of the candles in the darkness, with silence gently broken with spoken words and with music that has the rhythm and feeling of this cycle of light and darkness in our lives.

Symbols carry our meanings and beliefs—they carry them, they do not stand still with them. Symbols are not things we can put out on a table, take apart and study. They are things that we do, and thus they entwine themselves with our lives. Only then do they become symbols. Only then can they express what we mean and believe and strengthen in us true meaning and heartfelt belief.

The ritual that the church—the people assembled—does is as much ritual as a birthday party or an inauguration. But it differs from these other rituals, for what liturgy expresses in symbol is what these people believe and mean to be the very heart of their existence. Those who believe alike and belong to a common church may share certain things—structures of church government, a morality, a creed. But none of these can sustain community, can sustain faith. Only their ritual, their expressing in symbolic ways what they believe and mean, can do this.

1. The symbols that have carried Christian tradition for centuries and centuries have the power to do so because they are integral to our lives today. What symbols reflect most deeply the meanings and beliefs of your life? of the life of your family? of the life of your parish?

One who is convinced that symbol and reality are mutually exclusive should avoid the liturgy. Such a one should also avoid poetry, concerts and the theater, language, loving another person, and most other attempts at communicating with one's kind. Symbol is reality at its most intense degree of being expressed.

One resorts to symbol when reality swamps all other forms of discourse. This happens regularly when one approaches God with others, as in the liturgy. Symbol is thus as native to liturgy as metaphor is to language. One learns to live with symbol and metaphor or gives up the ability to speak or to worship communally.

Aidan Kavanagh

Ritual, symbol, sacrament and sacrifice all have a two-fold quality, which closely parallels our human situation. In their living state they have an outside and an inside, a visible action and an invisible action, both real, both needed, and so closely interdependent that each loses its true quality if torn apart; for indeed an idolatry which pins religion to abstract thoughts and notions alone is not much better than an idolatry which pins it to concrete stocks and stone alone. Either of these extremes are impoverishments, which destroy the true quality of a full and living cultus, wherein spirit and sense must constantly collaborate, as they do in all our significant acts and experiences.

Evelyn Underhill

Symbols That Carry the Tradition

he symbols with which the church expresses its prayer are not many, nor are they far removed from everyday human life. They are not unique to the Christian churches, but can be found in various forms in many societies. The most universal of these symbols is probably the sharing of a sacred meal, a rite of eating together that conveys and strengthens the unity of those partaking and their unity with their God. Within the Jewish tradition, the sacred meal has taken several forms, each drawing meanings from the history and faith of Israel. Such a rite is the Passover meal: a night when the people, gathered in their own homes and sharing with those in need, tell the same story, share the memories of the same sufferings and deliverance, affirm the same hope and partake of the same foods, which are themselves bound up with the story, liberation and hope.

Among the Jews there also developed a deep sense of the holiness of every meal, of food and table fellowship as constant occasions to praise and thank God. These occasions would normally be the meal of a family or household together, but sometimes they would be more formal, when larger groups of people who shared common bonds came together. Among the Jews the development of special rituals such as Passover and the more usual blessing of the household's meals has continued. For Christians, the memory of Jesus' last supper and of other occasions when he blessed and broke bread with his followers brought a new meaning to the Jewish ritual meal. The early church said that Christians gathered on the first day of the week for the "breaking of the bread." And through all the later ages, through misunderstandings and misinterpretations, the basic ritual continued: blessing bread and wine in the eucharistic prayer, that is, the prayer of thanksgiving, breaking the bread and sharing the bread and wine. Attitudes and emphases have varied through the ages, but the tradition continues. Christians express their faith and their common life through gathering at a table to give thanks over the bread and wine and to share the banquet of the Lord.

Ordinary food and drink, the thanksgiving-filled sharing of these, the eating and drinking together that is such a deep and common part of being human: These make up the ritual that continues to express our lives as Christians. Their roots are in hunger—for food, for each other, for the Lord. They are not something terribly theoretical, the realm of the mystic or theologian, but something we know about firsthand because they are so simple, so human.

Much the same is true for the other symbols that have carried our faith from generation to generation. The baptismal washing with water, the laying on of hands in blessing and healing and commissioning, the anointing with oil, the singing of praise to God morning and evening: These are marks of the church. These have carried the faith through centuries.

Nothing in the liturgical renewal of recent years has been about replacing these symbols with "contemporary" substitutes. Rather, the renewal is rooted in the realization that it is our fidelity to such basic rites that, beyond structures and creeds, gives identity to the church. The reform and renewal of our rites are efforts to free our symbols from things that keep them from doing their work: to free them from mechanical performance, from magic and superstition, from ministers who are assigned ministries without consideration of their gifts, from a spectator mentality. The renewal is about freeing our symbols to be what they mean to be—expressions of the living faith of people. The renewal is about the people—us—possessing the fullness of Christian prayer. The renewal is about a church whose communion meal, baptismal bath, laying on of hands in healing and forgiveness are the deepest expressions of who we have been, who we are now and who we hope to become.

Those who would work for good liturgy can sometimes think that it is an exercise in interpretation: educating people so that they can translate symbols into theological language. Not so. Good liturgy means that no explanations are needed, that the symbol and the story surrounding it are done fully, faithfully, powerfully. This happens when our rites, which are rooted in all that it means to be human, which tell all that it means to be Christian, are truly ours to do.

1. The basics of the Christian meal, the bread and the wine, are foods that are the result of much human effort and participation—reaping the grain, plucking grapes from the vine; kneading the dough, crushing the grapes. Consider how the ease of fast food separates you from the human work that goes into the food of the life of God in the church.

2. Our culture often leads us to believe that what is easier and faster is always better. How often do you forsake the kitchen work of chopping vegetables, mixing salads and even cleaning up for the ease of carry-out food? Does your faith pay a price for the conveniences of our culture?

To landscape the imagination; to feed and free it by the power-laden symbols of life and death, failure and finitude, absence and plenty, debt and grandeur: that is liturgy's redeeming work in and for the life of the world. Liturgy is what underwrites the social contract — and it is ultimately what shapes and conditions all love and enjoyment in our world.

Nathan Mitchell

"We are the body of Christ" — that living bread which delights our eyes and noses, fingers and tongues with its sweetness and variety. Delicate little white dinner rolls, crusty wholemeal cobs, heavy rye sourdough, baps, stotties, cottages, croissants — we are all there in any Sunday congregation. Looking too good to eat, we have come nevertheless to be snapped, torn, passed in pieces from hand to hand, to be bitten, savored, chewed and swallowed. To dwell in the belly of our neighbors in Christ, to pass into their tissues and sustain their life.

The richness you spread before us in your body reminds us of those great feasts in which your stories body forth the mighty promise of God. And yet, dear Christ, you come to us as tiny fragments, a wafer, a token nibble of the loaf; not even a mouthful, let alone a meal. Bread of affliction you offer us, starvation rations with a little desert dust in it. As you promised we find that it sustains us, we are no longer hungry. But we have not had enough. We trudge on through the wilderness, singing praises to you for this manna, holding out our invitations to the wedding feast.

But this is it! This is the wedding feast where your fullness and your desolation join hands and will not be parted, here in this bread which we break in your name, and this cup that you dare us to drink.

Jane Gaden

Symbols That Carry the Community

iturgy planners sometimes complain of how difficult good liturgy is in very large parishes, what with the crowds and the impersonal nature seemingly imposed by such numbers. Even in smaller churches people may feel that they have little in common, may feel no need to be a community in order to pray together. We can sometimes wonder if consistently good liturgy is compatible with circumstances today. Many people seem content with the mediocre; others just don't want any more "changes." But people who have experienced liturgy done well, with reverence and with care and with real celebration, may want very much for everyone to experience the depth of good liturgy regularly—but how can this happen?

Renewing the church's ritual will be a very long task. It has to be, for it cannot happen by decree or by simply reforming the liturgical books. Nor can it happen by itself, without efforts and movements that draw people to the gospel and toward belonging in a church and in a particular church community. Anyway, it just wouldn't be liturgy if it could be renewed by itself apart from all the quirkiness and messiness of people, of church. They, we, are what liturgy is all about.

But liturgy is an action of a community: people who share at least something of a history, a belonging to one another, a common suffering, a common hope. Liturgy in fact helps to create that community because it can be a deep affirmation of what we share, what binds us together. What seems to be clear, though, is that it is difficult for this affirmation to happen unless we are all very much at home with our ritual. The abilities that go into doing the Sunday parish eucharist well—by every member of the assembly—we do not become proficient with these if they are used only in the large gathering at the church. These things—how to sing in praise of God, how to be silent and reflect, how to listen to scripture, how to do our great prayer of thanksgiving—are best practiced in smaller groups.

The prayer of the larger community depends on the prayer of the little communities—couples and families and individuals. In fact, the support of such prayer must never be far from the concern of those who work in liturgy. Many forms of individual and household prayer once very familiar have disappeared and little has come to replace them. Our society does not encourage the attitudes or the time that prayer needs. But there is also little in contemporary society that satisfies the hunger for prayer once it is recognized.

We need this interdependence between the small group and the community. How can we own what we do at the eucharistic prayer and at holy communion unless we experience in the day-to-day course of our lives the giving of praise and thanks to God for our food and for fellowship? This is a matter not only of prayer at table, but of everything that happens at table: of the care we take in this matter of sharing, the thanks we give for food and each other, the ways we attend to one another's needs, the reverence we have for the fruit of the earth and the work of human hands. How can we own the psalms as processional and reflective chants in the Sunday liturgy if at least a few of the psalms are not a staple of the prayer of adults and children alike? Can song be integral to Sunday liturgy if it is not integral to prayer at home?

At home, whether one person alone or many together, we practice the skills of our ritual—the stuff that makes our liturgy. The symbols of our liturgy, like thanksgiving and eating, are linked to life in our body, our spirit, our day to-day movement from birth to death. Here, in the heart of each person, are the rhythms of prayer and ritual that need to come together with the larger church.

1. When we think about the long and slow task that is the renewing of the church's ritual, it can seem daunting and the thought of participating can seem overwhelming. But changes are incremental, and they happen by each person's willingness to take on a small part of the long task. Think about talking to the coordinator of liturgical ministries in your parish about what you might contribute to the reform.

2. For all of the wonders of our culture, it is not one that supports that tradition of sharing food and life around the table with those we love, with those we are committed to. In what ways might you change the meal tradition of your table so that those in your home would be more prepared for approaching the table of the Lord?

Seriousness and earnestness about symbols has nothing to do with somberness or lugubriousness. Liturgy is festivity and fantasy and play. Play is to be taken seriously but not somberly. The Christian who would serve liturgical renewal and make public worship serve its purpose must learn how to play — against all of his capitalist and rationalist instincts. This is not as easy as it sounds, and its difficulty accounts for the fact that many priests and liturgical leaders who are trying to be progressive and helpful are really neither. Carelessness is not the same as play. Sloppiness is not the same as festivity.

Robert W. Hovda

❖

And Sunday after Sunday, we nourish a hope, faint and often unfulfilled, that our worship will take us to places of beauty and meaning we do not normally inhabit, places we have helped to create, places we will return from, refreshed and whole. "Where there is no vision," Proverbs reminds us, "the people perish" (29:18). We come to this setting to hear the sacred story and pray the great prayer with sisters and brothers, hoping to feel enlarged, expansive, full of praise, better than we are, knowing this is the way God sees us in Christ Jesus.

Virginia Sloyan

The Elements of Liturgy

Taking apart good liturgy to see what makes it run always yields an incomplete answer. Although in liturgy the whole is greater than the sum of its parts, we here look at the various elements to understand how we can best do them.

Awareness of our own humanity — its daily words, ordinary gestures, songs we sing and spaces in which we live and work — deepens our participation in the mystery of the incarnation. So we look at some of these "ordinary" aspects of liturgy: word, movement, music and environment. These elements do their work most clearly when we respect their limits and their possibilities. They flow through all our church ritual and most of our other rites as well, for they are basic to human expression.

Word: 1
The Ways We Use Words in Liturgy

 ometimes the renewal of the liturgy since Vatican II seems to have reduced the liturgy to words. In many places, the times when silence is called for are short, and there is speaking from beginning to end. Sometimes the words of the prayers and scriptures are added to not only with a homily but also with frequent and verbose explanations and reminders of the theme of the liturgy. We know that the Latin liturgy before the reform was capable of being not only impressive but also prayerful — in spite of the fact that not a single word would have been intelligible to the assembly. We know that liturgy does not work by words alone. More than this, we know that if we act as if it does, as if the liturgy were all words, then what we would damage most is the words themselves.

Words in liturgy are not like words on the evening news, or words in the lecture hall, or words in the store or office. What are they like? There are ways we use words in other rituals in life that show something of how words work in liturgy.

Consider the greetings and the acclamations. We have rituals to get us through moments of greeting one another. "How are you?" "Good to see you again!" "What's up?" Or simply: "Good morning!" We also have ritual words for parting. Such words are often accompanied by a gesture: a wave, a handshake, a kiss. The content of such ritual words of greeting and parting hardly matters: They are formulas. Does that mean they are insincere? Not at all! Is it insincere to play a role, to speak a line? Is Kenneth Branagh insincere when he becomes Hamlet? Obviously, a person can give an insincere greeting, can be miles away instead of present to that person, but the words are the same. They are formulas we have, formulas that have stayed with us for generations, for easing the first and last moments we have together. It is the same with these words in liturgy. They are formulas, and they can be made empty and insincere or they can be filled with our presence. These words usually belong to the presider and to the assembly. "The grace and peace . . ." "Amen." "The Lord be with you." "And also with you." "Go in peace." "Thanks be to God." We play a

role, speak a line, when we say these, but that is what gives them their great potential.

Another ritual way to use words is acclamation. Acclamations are by their nature for everybody. They are the "Hooray!" and the "Viva!" of the liturgy. They are ritual words like "Alleluia," "Amen" and "Holy, holy, holy." In the flow of liturgy they have to be acclaimed with great strength — and so nearly always they should be sung. There will be more detail about this in the articles on music.

There are other ways we use words in liturgy. There are the prayers led by the presider. At Mass, these are the opening prayer, the prayer over the gifts, the eucharistic prayer and the prayer after communion. These are nearly always addressed to the Father and often need moments of silence to prepare for them. They are spoken by one in the name of all present. They are words of the church that are rooted in the words of the scriptures and our tradition. They are formal. As time goes on, the English-language prayers will grow for us into beloved prayers of great beauty, with words that bear the weight of repetition and open ever-new meanings to those who hear them.

Litanies are another ritual use of words. Chanting serves their nature very well, for litanies build on constant repetition of a refrain. At Mass, the penitential rite is often cast in the form of a litany; the prayers of intercession and the "Lamb of God" are also litanies.

Words of invitation are used at liturgy. "Let us pray," "Let us give thanks," and the invitations to join in prayers of intercession, to exchange the peace greeting and to join in communion are all words of this kind. The invitation helps to center attention, call us together and point us toward what we are about to do.

Words in liturgy have all sorts of uses. In planning graceful and strong liturgy for the community, it helps to know precisely how words are being used.

Stepping back from the liturgy itself from time to time to ponder the various words of the liturgy can help us refocus the intentionality that we must all bring to the liturgy so that our community's liturgy can be filled with our active and conscious participation.

Many of the words we use at liturgy are repeated frequently, either within the same act of worship or from week to week. Using these words again and again makes us feel at home with them. Familiarity with them can free us to pray better. But there is also a danger with ritual words. We can become so used to them that they lose their meaning and become empty and lifeless to us unless we make a conscious effort to put our spirit into them.

1. Are there some common ritual words that seem to have become mechanical in your community? Some that are particularly alive and intense?

2. Can music help your words? How? *Slower*

3. What values have you experienced in your use of ritual words?

4. Are there steps that can help prevent boredom and rote repetition in the liturgy?

The Hebrew word for "word" is *dabar* which means "deed" (an action) as well as "word." By this definition, words are not merely sounds or symbols that describe deeds but are themselves deeds. Our tendency at this point might be to see such an association as merely poetic. But "word as deed" is not an understanding found only in the highly intuitive thought characteristic of the Middle East, where our scriptures were born. Language scholars in the contemporary West have formulated a similar view. They have demonstrated that words are not always just sounds or written symbols that refer to something, as in "There is the house I live in." In some usages, words actually do something, and in these cases they are called "performative speech acts." A simple example: The words "I baptize you," or "I forgive you," or "Bless you!" do not simply refer to actions; they actually accomplish the actions they describe.

Aelred Rosser

❖

To do justice to the mystery of Easter joy with the stale words of human speech is rather difficult. This is so not only because every mystery of the gospel penetrates only with difficulty into the narrow confines of human life — thereby making it even harder for our words to grasp and contain and express these mysteries — but because the Easter message is the most human tidings of Christianity. That is why we find it the most difficult message to understand. For what is most true, most obvious and most easy, is the most difficult to be, to do and to believe. That is to say, modern people base life on the unexpressed, and therefore all the more self-evident, prejudice that anything "religious" is merely an affair of the most interior heart and of the loftiest spirit — something that we must bring about by ourselves, something, therefore that involves the difficulties and unreality of the heart's thoughts and moods.

Karl Rahner

Word: 2
Scripture and Reflection

henever the church gathers, we share stories about the meaning of life and about humanity's long walk with God. These stories help us to understand God's continuing presence with us and for us. In the telling of these sacred stories, we hear God's voice. And the church responds to this ever-present God. At very short prayers, as at mealtime, our response may be in the form of a few words that echo some song or prayer of the scriptures. But at eucharist, at reconciliation, at the anointing of the sick, weddings, morning and evening prayer and at funerals, the scriptures are present as the fundamental element—that is, the foundation—of the liturgy.

How do we think about scripture, these words from the church's book, in the liturgy? As the retelling of the story of our life with God.

The popular searching for roots makes us all aware that there is a story that connects us with our past and tells us much of our personal history, a story that identifies us among all the peoples of the earth. Any tribe of people that remains closely bound together does so in great part because of the story that they continue to tell to explain to themselves and to their children who they are. Such a story most often involves a whole view of the world, including the relations among creatures and the place of the gods. No matter how sophisticated our society, we do not lose this need for common story, as can be seen in the stories retold around national holidays.

There is also the universal phenomenon of fairy tales. They form a worldwide language in which adults pass on to the next generation the common story of all humankind: the struggle of good and evil, the suffering of the innocent, things that happen that are beyond our control, the coming vindication of the good. Stories talk about such things in a way that touches the mind and heart and spirit.

And that is basically why we continue to read the scriptures. We grow up into the cycle of stories of faith. The story may be shaped as a narrative or it may be a song, a genealogy, a set of laws, an exhortation, a vision, a warning, a parable, a prophecy. These are the makings of the larger story. On most Sundays, we read bit by bit, more or less in order, through one of the gospels and also through the other apostolic writings, the letters. When a special occasion is observed, some parts of our story that revolve around that day are read. Often the reading from the Hebrew scriptures sounds a note that is echoed in that day's gospel reading. (This does not mean that the first is merely a preparation and the second the reality. The church has clearly said that the validity of the Hebrew scriptures is not changed by the existence of the gospels and other apostolic writings. Rather, the gospels echo the Hebrew scripture, as when the gospel tells of Jesus curing a deaf man after the Hebrew Scripture has spoken of the reign of God as a time when the deaf will hear. This shows us that we Christians need to know the Hebrew scriptures. Jesus and the apostles knew them deeply. If we are to understand their words and lives, we must make their scriptures our own.)

In many tribes, the grandparents, the elders, are the ones who tell the story at times of festivity or at times of sorrow. They have lived the story most deeply in their own lives; they know that the story in fact tells their lives better than an autobiography would, tells the group's life at a level deeper than facts and dates and places. This storytelling, of course, is not necessarily a function of age. We entrust the telling of our story to people, elders or not, who can capture and keep the attention of the assembly, whose lives reflect their love of our scriptures, who are deeply aware of just how this story and this people belong together.

Another use of words in liturgy, one always related to scripture, is the homily. Homilists reflect on our lives and our times in light of the story that we have heard. Words in the homily are not scholarly explanations of scripture, nor pious exhortations, nor rambling personal notes. A homily may be cast in one of many styles, but its purpose is always to let the way the scripture has touched the speaker echo in the listeners and link them all, speaker and listeners together, to the mystery being celebrated.

1. Once a little girl said to her aunt: "Tell me again how my daddy told his first grade teacher that he wanted to go home, and she thought he said he had to go to the bathroom so she said, 'Go,' and he left school and started walking home. But then he came to the street and remembered he wasn't allowed to cross the street without his big sister, so he stood there crying. And that's where you found him and brought him back to school." Obviously she knew the story! What she wanted was an elder to tell it again.

2. Although we hear the scriptures every time we gather for prayer, it takes a long time for them to be part of our lives. We want the word to be effective for all at liturgy. Can we help the scriptures be more intelligible through nonliturgical channels such as the parish bulletin and adult education? Besides the homily, how can the scriptures be more a part of our parish community's life?

3. Here is a technique some small Christian communities use to break open the meaning of a scripture passage, especially a gospel pericope. Read the Sunday gospel before you go to Mass and ask yourself these questions as you read. This technique can be very helpful.

    (a) Who is in the text? What are they doing? Why are they doing it?

    (b) What is going on in the text?

    (c) What does this text make me feel? Why?

    (d) What bothers or annoys or makes me nervous in this story? Why?

    (e) What in the text gives me hope?

    (f) What "belief statements" come to me from this text?

    (g) What lesson have I learned from this text?

    (h) Is there a way to put this lesson into practice?

The reading and homily are meant to stir up the hearer so that, to borrow a phrase from Saint Augustine's work on Christian instruction, "he to whom you speak may by hearing come to faith, by believing come to hope, and by hoping come to love" (*First Catechetical Instruction*, n. 4). This is not a time, then, for giving instruction in Christian doctrine, but for awakening the faith, hope and love of the people of God that they may proclaim, in word and ritual, the mystery of faith.

Mark Searle

To have a comprehensive knowledge of the social, political and economic forces shaping the contemporary world, while at the same time specializing in scriptural exegesis and theology and being pastorally competent may well appear to be an overwhelming, even impossible, expectation to lay on any one person.

The point to be made here, however, is not that preachers must know everything, but rather that there is no limit to the sources of knowledge and insight that a preacher can draw upon. There are many avenues which lead toward a deeper understanding of the human condition. Some will travel more easily down the avenue of the social sciences, others down the avenue of literature and the arts, others down the avenue of popular culture. What ultimately matters is not which avenue we take, but what we take with us as we travel.

Fulfilled in Your Hearing, *35*

Movement: 1
Our Tradition of Body and Prayer

ry to have a ritual sometime without moving. At a birthday party, nobody lights the candles, nobody blows them out, nobody claps after singing "Happy Birthday to You!" At the St. Patrick's Day parade, no marching, no raising a glass. Before the baseball game, no standing or removing hats for the national anthem. Even if you somehow planned a motionless ritual, something like a yoga meditation with everyone sitting very still and silent, then the very motionlessness would become a ritual in which no words are spoken and in which there is no music of any kind. To do something important and something shared among people without using the body in ritual is unimaginable to us.

In discussing the ways we use our bodies in our prayer together, we find obvious differences. Sometimes religious rituals involve much spontaneous movement. Some Pentecostal churches have made this especially important, encouraging people to manifest the Spirit in jumping, clapping and dancing. There are some parts of the Catholic church where rituals have evolved that allow such bodily expression. However, such spontaneous movement is not part of the religious experience of most Christians of European background. Many who would not welcome this type of spontaneous movement at worship would, however, consider it the correct thing to do in other settings, say, at a political rally or a football game.

Whether or not we experience spontaneous, vigorous bodily movement in liturgy, we all participate in more moderate movements in our common prayer. Catholics have developed and preserved certain gestures as a vital part of our worship. Consider genuflecting, the various ways of making the sign of the cross, kneeling and standing, striking the breast, bowing the head at the name of Jesus, folding the hands and the gestures of taking communion in the hand and drinking from the cup. These are common to everyone. We also know the gestures that go especially with the ministry of the presider: extending the arms, raising the hands, deep bows, blessing gestures and gestures associated with various objects, such as swinging the censer, kissing the gospel book, raising the bread and cup. Some of these gestures, such as the extended hands and deep bows, historically belonged to the whole assembly but gradually fell into disuse as the assembly's participation in the liturgy dwindled in times past.

Because of this history, liturgical gestures sometimes seem to be private: Gestures seem to be reduced, done mechanically and without thought, without grace. To bring the vigor into liturgical gesture that it rightfully deserves usually includes two elements: deliberateness and fullness. When a person consciously and deliberately makes a gesture, his or her attention is focused on that gesture, and the gesture's meaning becomes present and clear to the person making it. When people allow their bodies to enter into the gesture fully, their experience of the meaning of the action is enhanced.

Common gesture in our worship involves each person, each whole person, body and mind and spirit, in the prayer. Common gesture is a way to manifest that this is the prayer and action of a *church*—the one body of Christ. Even more, common gesture in worship helps to bring this about.

This is not, of course, a matter of just any gesture done just any way. Graceful, conscious, full gestures show respect for the body, a respect resounding from deep within a church that believes in the Incarnation; without such gestures, the praying is muted and obscured.

"The liturgy of the Church has been rich in a tradition of ritual movement and gestures. These actions, subtly, yet really, contribute to an environment which can foster prayer or which can distract from prayer. When the gestures are done in common, they contribute to the unity of the worshiping assembly." (Bishops' Committee on the Liturgy, *Environment and Art in Catholic Worship*, 56)

1. What bodily rituals that bring you in touch with other people do you go through from the time you awake until the beginning of the first task of the day?

2. Name a few of your family gestures (think broadly).

3. What gestures are you comfortable with in prayer? Has this changed through the years?

4. Are there liturgical gestures that your community could be more intentional about this year?

5. How can you incorporate more gesture into your Sunday worship?

The body is meant . . . for the Lord, and the Lord for the body. And God raised the Lord and will also raise us by his power. Do you not know that your bodies are members of Christ? Anyone united to the Lord becomes one spirit with him. . . . Do you not know that your body is the temple of the Holy Spirit within you, which you have from God, and that you are not your own? For you were bought with a price; therefore glorify God in your body.

1 Corinthians 6:13 – 15, 17, 19 – 20

Our hands may also indicate the goods we lack — our unchecked impulses, our distractions, and other faults. Let us hold them as the Church directs and see to it that there is a real correspondence between the interior and exterior attitude.

In matters such as this we are on delicate ground. We would prefer not to talk about things of this order. Something within us objects. Let us then avoid all empty and unreal talk and concentrate the more carefully on the actual doing. That is a form of speech by which the plain realities of the body say to God what its sound means and intends.

Romano Guardini

Movement: 2
From Here to There

he way a minister or the whole assembly gets from here to there during the liturgy is a good illustration of what happens in a ritual when something practical has to be done. The presider in the back of the room, having greeted people as they arrived for the liturgy, now needs to be in front to welcome everyone and lead the opening prayer: A procession is needed. The deacon is at the chair and it is time for the gospel: a procession. The people are in their places and it is time to share communion: another procession.

But processions sometimes happen for their own sake—on Palm Sunday, Corpus Christi, the feast of a patron saint. There is festivity and display, and the procession itself may be the ritual.

Getting from here to there in a ritual manner—for a practical purpose or to have a good time or to display something important—happens frequently outside religious rituals. A rite where such movement is the main means of expression is a parade. In a good parade, one could never say that the participants are only the people on the floats and in the bands: Rather, the celebrants include these and everyone else along the way. Everyone is swept into the festivity. The occasion of a parade might be a display of ethnic pride, the ritual movement of a newly inaugurated president from the Capitol to the White House, the beginning of the holiday shopping season in Thanksgiving Day parades, the memory of an event as in Memorial Day parades, or even a vision of a better society as in a Labor Day parade.

There are simpler sorts of parades and processions to get people with some special part to play from here to there. Think of the entrance procession of the players at an athletic contest, for example, or the arrival of movie stars on opening night, or the entrance of a judge into the courtroom. Some processions seem to happen in similar ways whether the ritual is given any religious meaning by its participants or not: for instance, the procession of the bride (and perhaps the groom) to the place where the vows will be exchanged, or the procession (in cars or on foot) behind the casket when someone is being buried.

We all have some feeling for when processions are effective and when they are not. We all know something about how a procession that is done only once a year can be handled, and how different a procession that happens every Sunday must be. We can recognize the elements that make these processions work. The way certain presiders enter the worship space is in itself a powerful statement about who we are and why we are here—and why is that? Why can others take the same path and end up in the same place and nothing at all is felt about the who or the why? At the gospel, one way of doing the procession proclaims that we are to rise and acclaim the good news and another way leaves people wondering if they are supposed to stand—and why is that? Why does the reception of holy communion sometimes looks like a bunch of people shuffling up for a private exchange with the minister, and other times looks like a community sharing one meal, the body and blood of Christ?

An expressive procession is not just a matter of executing a decision: "We will have a procession. So-and-so will go with Father from here to there." It is a matter of timing. A matter of pace. A matter of bearing. A matter of grace. A matter of reverence. A matter of space. A matter of sensing what this particular procession is about: Entrance processions are not like gospel processions; communion processions are not like exit processions. Each has its own character. This is important only at eucharist, but at special celebrations like weddings, funerals and baptisms.

> Processions are for the people who move and who like to be moved, for people who have strong religious convictions and like to show them, for people who—by training, experience or intuition—know how much the body in its simple movement of walking brings to the mind and to the spirit in fostering religious experience. Processions are for people who have a sense for symbolic gestures and a feel that the correlations of feet (which walk) and hands (which carry palms, flowers, song sheets, rosaries, candles) and voices (which sing and pray), that this harmonizing of three existential signs creates a very strong and supporting pattern of witnessing and praise. (Regina Kuehn in *Liturgy 70*, February 1978)

1. Rituals tend either to order our lives or disorder them. Consider your rituals in getting from home to church and back home again. Do they order your life? What quality, positive or not, do they add to your life?

2. List the various processions in your community's worship experience. Don't forget wedding processions, funeral processions, processions to the font, processions for ashes or candles or palms. What makes a good procession good? What is it that can make processions lifeless and unappealing? What effect might changes in music, color, choice of participants, banners or route make? Could some processions go outside the church building?

3. Is there one procession that needs work in your community? What improvements could be made? What things need to be learned to make those improvements?

What is procession?

It is journey distilled — journey at its heart,

a gathering into one movement

of a church on the way:

a pilgrim people, a dusty, longing people

yet walking with heads high;

knowing ourselves, showing ourselves

to be the royal nation, the holy people

won by the Son,

called by his word,

gathered around his table.

There we discover again,

from age to age, from east to west,

for all our journeys,

the source, the ground, the companion, the way.

Janet Schlichting

❖

Liturgical formation . . . will not be the creation of ownership nor the taming of the symbols, but rather the passing on of polarity. It will involve a welcome to *here* that is always open to *there*, an invitation that does not forget the warning, a warning always paired with invitation. If juxtaposition is the key characteristic of the *ordo*, if Christian worship speaks truthfully about God by always speaking at least two words, two things together, then welcome to the interactions of the meeting will be marked by the same two-ness.

Gordon Lathrop

Movement: 3
How Does It Work?

ovement in liturgical celebration can be categorized into three areas: posture (how and when we stand, sit and kneel), processions and gestures. Let us look at the Sunday Mass, since that is our most familiar ritual, and see these movements at work.

Posture. Meanings are not arbitrarily assigned to postures. We know from our own experience what meaning a posture has for us, yet we also know that in one culture, for example, sitting may mean reverence, while in another, it is standing that expresses this. We know other things, too: that changing quickly from one posture to another and back again is only distracting; that an assembly that celebrates liturgy regularly does not need to be told to sit, to stand or to kneel. Posture accomplishes (or does not) two things in ritual: our posture expresses and strengthens our devotion (which is why, for example, we usually stand up to cheer), and our posture keeps a good rhythm during the ritual (which is why we have a seventh-inning stretch).

Sitting, for us, is for resting, listening or watching. What moments at Mass call for sitting? What is kneeling for? For sorrow? For adoration? Is there something about kneeling that makes a moment more private, more inward? What about standing? We stand to greet people or to honor someone; we stand when we are filled with excitement.

Now at Mass on a particular Sunday we may not feel like listening at this moment, or like acclaiming at another. But at liturgy, all present give themselves to the ritual, enter into the prayer. The postures we take can, over the long term, help the ritual do its work, can help prayer to happen in a very real way. How we sit, how we stand, how we kneel—these are important to the spirit of the liturgy. This is even more true for ministers, whose posture can inspire (or annoy) the people who see them. We know that sloppiness is contagious; we know that care and reverence are too.

Processions. We have a feeling for what is unique to each procession in the Sunday liturgy: the entrance procession, gospel, preparation of gifts, communion, exit. Who is involved in each procession? How have they prepared for their role in the procession? Carrying objects gracefully and with reverence, candles or crosses or books or plates—and carrying oneself gracefully and with reverence—some people can do these easily, and some people need to practice. The presence of auxiliary ministers at communion was primarily intended to clarify the meaning of this rite: one meal. But the arrangement of the ministers and the way the procession happens can obscure this. Each procession can help the ritual to be deeply prayerful. How?

And *gestures.* Those with specific ministries have more gestures to do than the assembly has. The server learns how and when to bow, and honors the altar with a graceful gesture of respect and adoration. The lector learns to hold the book high, and honors our sacred scriptures in a dignified gesture of exaltation. The presider makes gestures of welcome as he speaks the words of greeting, and gathers the assembly into community with his eyes, hands, arms—with his whole person. For these gestures to resound in our liturgy, we need to practice, to learn from others, to be aware of what these gestures feel like as we do them fully and consciously. The assembly, too, has its gestures: The assembly makes the sign of of the cross as a conscious gesture of true community; the assembly raises hands in praise and blessing, clasps hands in peace and unity, bows heads to ask for and receive God's blessing.

This is difficult. There is much in our culture that wants us to be passive spectators; that wants us to be embarrassed if a genuflection reveals adoration or raised hands show praise; that distracts us from being fully aware and thoughtful about what we are doing right now, as we do it. But those things would prevent us from entering into our ritual, our liturgy, as whole people. And only whole people can enter into ritual fully.

1. Ministers can model conscious, deliberate gestures in many ways. A cantor can invite the assembly to stand by slowly and deliberately raising her arms while looking directly at the people's faces. All the ministers, including young altar servers, can reverence the altar by gracefully and prayerfully bending their bodies in a deep bow. The community's sign of the cross is a full, conscious and prayerful gesture when all the ministers at the altar make the sign slowly, boldly and deliberately.

2. Make a list of the gestures and postures used by the assembly and ministers and think about them. How would you describe the appropriateness, the gracefulness and the prayerfulness of each of these bodily movements? Which are especially beautiful in your community? Are there any that need some attention?

3. If it seems that a certain gesture is done without as much awareness as some others, you can bring it to the attention of the community in many ways. For instance, supplement the Sunday bulletin with an explanation of the gesture, bowing, for example. Explain how to do the gesture fully and gracefully, and include the meanings that Christians through the ages have found in this gesture. Good illustrations will help; after all, a picture is worth a thousand words. It is helpful to follow up the bulletin article in various ways, including an encouraging word from the presider at announcement time. Make sure that all ministers, in their initial training and regular refreshers, are encouraged to incorporate this gesture appropriately and well whenever they are present at the liturgy, whether they are exercising their ministry or not.

When we cross ourselves, let it be with a real sign of the cross. Instead of a small cramped gesture that gives no notion of its meaning, let us make a large unhurried sign from forehead to breast, from shoulder to shoulder, consciously feeling how it includes the whole of us — our thoughts, our attitudes, our body and soul, every part of us at once — how it consecrates and sanctifies us.

It does so because it is the sign of the universe and the sign of our redemption. On the cross Christ redeemed humankind. By the cross he sanctifies us to the last shred and fiber of our being. We make the sign of the cross before we pray to collect and compose ourselves and to fix our minds and hearts and wills upon God. We make it when we finish praying in order that we may hold fast the gift we have received from God. In temptations we sign ourselves to be strengthened; in dangers, to be protected. The cross is signed upon us in blessings in order that the fullness of God's life may flow into the soul and fructify and sanctify us wholly.

Think of these things when you make the sign of the cross. It is the holiest of all signs. Make a large cross, taking time, thinking about what you do. Let it take in your whole being — body, soul, mind, will, thoughts, feelings, your doing and not-doing — and by signing it with the cross strengthen and consecrate the whole in the strength of Christ, in the name of the triune God.

Romano Guardini

Music: I
The Sound of Our Prayer

hat is the sound of people at prayer? We can begin to answer that question by thinking about the sounds of other human assemblies. What are the sounds of people at a banquet? What are the sounds of people at a horse race? What are the sounds of a PTA meeting? What are the sounds of an auction? What are the sounds of a classroom? What are the sounds of a political convention? What do human voices do, other than communicate information, in these various situations? If you heard tape recordings of any of these without identification, could you name that assembly?

What people do with their voices is a vital part of any occasion. The association between situations and their sounds becomes inseparable: Can you imagine watching a movie of a horse race with the sound track of a funeral?

But what is the sound of people engaged in doing liturgy together? We are still learning. The patterns of our liturgy that were established for hundreds of years—up until less than a lifetime ago—had the priest performing nearly all the active parts in the liturgy. The people were spectators, from whom few sounds were expected. The sounds of the liturgy then were words murmured by one voice in Latin, a small bell ringing, the tabernacle door closing, the censer jingling against its chain, the cruets clicking against the chalice, the shuffling of people standing and kneeling. Perhaps there was music from a choir or an organist.

Now, however, almost forty years after the Second Vatican Council, we have a new appreciation of what liturgy sounds like. We know that some sounds do not make for liturgical prayer, for instance, the "read-together" service, with priest and people alike following along in their books reading their lines. We also know that singing three or four hymns in the course of the Mass does not necessarily change things; this can give an impression of "And now, let's stop and sing a song."

The sounds we make in prayer should be integral to the prayer; the sounds we make are, in fact, how prayer gets into the voice. That is not just a matter of saying words. It is a matter of sounds. We do not sing to communicate information or to repeat facts: We sing because there is life and

faith and church. In liturgy, we can rejoice, we can be troubled, we can remember, we can hope. We can shatter the flatness of ordinary life. Liturgy calls for sounds—from our voices and instruments that people have made, from bells and hands clapping and feet walking. It calls for sounds that can be louder and softer, higher and lower, faster and slower than everyday speech. The liturgy does not have gaps that we need to fill with singing. Rather, singing, in various forms, is what we do to to express and embody our faith.

In their statement on music in the liturgy, the United States bishops said this:

> Music should assist the assembled believers to express and share the gift of faith that is within them and to nourish and strengthen their interior commitment of faith. It should heighten the texts so that they speak more fully and more effectively. The quality of joy and enthusiasm which music adds to community worship cannot be gained in any other way. It imparts a sense of unity to the congregation and sets the appropriate tone for a particular celebration. . . . Music can also unveil a dimension of meaning and feeling, a communication of ideas and intuitions which words alone cannot yield. (*Music in Catholic Worship*, 23–24)

Our need for this "quality of joy and enthusiasm" means that it is vital that we have a feeling for the sound of our prayer. This having a feeling for the sound does not mean whether or not a piece is rendered well, although that is important. It means that the sound creates a mood, expresses and deepens an attitude. Musicians can facilitate this sound by playing the organ and other instruments, by helping the assembly sing, by training large and small choirs who contribute their own sounds to the common prayer.

Music surrounds us today. Fine music is more accessible for more of us than at any other time in history. The kinds of music that can be heard are many and marvelously varied. More than ever, people are interested in doing music, in playing instruments, in singing. We are not always listeners. The sound of people praying is grand when we are aware of our need for music and have leaders who can help us release the power of our sound.

1. Choosing music for worship is not just a matter of finding words to match the texts of the day. The mood of a piece influences worship just as much as if not more than the words. List some examples from your community's experience.

2. Sometimes the instrument used for a piece of music can suggest a particular mood that another instrument could not. If "For All the Saints" were used at the end of a funeral liturgy with a full brass choir accompaniment, it would certainly create a different mood than if it were accompanied by a single flute. Examples?

3. Do the people sing the liturgy? Discuss that while thinking about the three words, *people, sing, liturgy.*

4. If so, come up with some reasons why, so that nothing will inadvertently be done to interfere with that.

5. If not, what could be done to help people sing the liturgy? What could be done to help people want to sing the liturgy?

6. How can we make sure that our convictions about music and liturgy are accurately reflected in the parish budget?

I say rediscovery, for here is what St. Ignatius of Antioch, writing about the year 108, tells the Ephesians about how they should pray in common: "Yes, one and all, you should form yourselves into a choir; so that in perfect harmony, and taking your pitch from God, you may sing in true unison and with one voice, as strings of a harp, to the Father through Jesus Christ."

Godfrey Diekmann

❖

Sing lustily and with a good courage. Beware of singing as if you were half dead, or half asleep; but lift up your voice with strength. Be no more afraid of your voice now, nor more ashamed of its being heard, than when you sang the songs of Satan.

John Wesley

Music: 2
Musical and Pastoral Judgments

he United States Bishops' Committee on the Liturgy issued official statements in 1972 (*Music in Catholic Worship*—MCW) and in 1982 (*Liturgical Music Today*—LMT) about the role of music in the liturgy. These important documents provide a solid approach to good liturgy.

The bishops propose three criteria for music in the liturgy: It is to be good music, it is to be pastorally suitable, and it is to do the work that the liturgy calls for. Here we will consider the first two of these judgments.

The bishops ask: "Is the music technically, aesthetically and expressively good?" The importance given to this judgment is backed up: "This judgment is basic and primary and should be made by competent musicians" (MCW 26).

Because worship is an activity of the whole person, because it is meant to engage us in spirit and in mind, in body and in heart and in soul, the elements of worship are those human arts that touch us deeply, in every part of our lives. The place of music in such an activity is obvious. More than any other means of human expression, music can convey any human emotion, conviction, humor, remembrance. Music is universal, an important part of every life.

Our tradition has used the collection of songs known as psalms since long before the time of Jesus. To this collection, the early church added new words and melodies to express their own experiences of the Lord. Over the centuries, the peoples of many cultures contributed music for the church to sing. In the best times we had strong music that everyone could sing, along with other music to be sung or played by those with gifts and special training. Local churches supported and encouraged the work of the talented musicians in their midst.

It is to the best of our musical tradition that the church is now called. At every level, the musical judgment is to be made by competent, trained musicians. The document explains: "Only artistically sound music will be effective in the long run. To admit the cheap, the trite, the musical cliché often found in popular songs on the grounds of instant liturgy is to cheapen the liturgy, to expose it to ridicule and to invite failure. Musicians must search for and create music of quality for worship.... They must... find new uses for the best of the old music. They must explore the repertory of good music used in other communions. They must find practical means of preserving and using our rich heritage of Latin chants and motets" (MCW 26–27).

Musical judgment is aware of another factor: It is important not to confuse style with value. Because worship takes its shape through art forms, it is necessary to choose over and over again among examples of various styles.

The musicians who best minister to the praying church are those who are able to sense which examples of which styles enhance prayer, assist the local church in its sound and encourage the words and melodies of the liturgy to extend into people's lives. Beyond being well-trained in music, then, the musician entrusted with this judgment by the local church must be sensitive to tastes and abilities, and open to a variety of styles of good music. This, in effect, is what the document calls the pastoral judgment.

"[The pastoral judgment] is the judgment that must be made in this particular situation, in these concrete circumstances. Does music in the celebration enable these people to express their faith, in this place, in this age, in this culture?" (39) In order to exercise pastoral judgment, the musician must work closely with others who have responsibility for the community's worship and must listen closely to the people of the community, listening for what is really meant, which can sometimes be hidden beneath what is said.

The musical and pastoral judgments are not only about the quality of the music that is selected. They are also about competence in their use. On the parish level, that can mean searching out volunteers with certain gifts, or guiding volunteers toward other ministries where their gifts fit better. But the goal is clear: good music that is well executed, forming a strong expression of this parish's faith.

Good music does not just happen. It takes good musicians with good instruments and a realistic budget to nurture good music at worship. It is unfair to expect a volunteer without formal training to be able to provide everything we desire of music at liturgy. Either we budget for further training, or we hire professional liturgical musicians to undertake the ministry of music. Every parish that is serious about good liturgy must also be serious about its musical budget. Good instruments, good musicians and sufficient books and scores are necessary.

1. How does your parish ensure that all three judgments (musical, pastoral and liturgical) are employed in planning liturgy?

2. Who makes the final judgment about the music to be used for liturgy?

3. How much variety is there in the music you use? How much familiarity?

4. What is the parish music budget? How often is it revised? How do you assure a just wage for your professional musicians?

5. How do you support the assembly's understanding and appreciation of music at liturgy?

Music is not an embellishment or a "gloss" on ritual activity; it is an intrinsic aspect of ritual activity itself. To put it another way, music is just as essential a part of the environment of Christian worship as presider and people, altar and font, plants and banners, candles and crosses.

Nathan Mitchell

Singing is the most human, most companionable of the arts. It joins us together in the whole realm of sound, forging a group identity where there were only individuals and making a communicative statement that far transcends what any one of us could do alone. It is a paradigm of union with the creator. It is what the words talk about. We *need* to sing well.

Alice Parker

The treasury of sacred music is to be preserved and cultivated with great care. Choirs must be diligently developed, especially in cathedral churches. Bishops and other pastors of souls must do their best to ensure that whenever a liturgical action is to be accompanied by chant, the whole body of the faithful may be able to take that active part which is rightly theirs.

Constitution on the Sacred Liturgy, *114*

Music: 3
Liturgical Judgment

ot all music that is good, not even all music that is good for this assembly, is necessarily good music for this assembly at this moment in this particular liturgy. For the liturgy makes its own demands. *Music in Catholic Worship* sums it up: "The nature of the liturgy itself will help to determine what kind of music is called for, what parts are to be preferred for singing and who is to sing them" (30). In *Liturgical Music Today,* the bishops remind us that "the entire worshiping assembly exercises a ministry of music" (63).

"What kind of music is called for" points to the need to explore specific moments in the liturgy. In a liturgy of the word, whether at Mass or on other occasions, there is need for music that is supportive but not demanding, music that allows the images called forth by the proclamation of the scriptures and nourished in silence to find expression in familiar refrains sung in alternation with verses are sung by the cantor or choir.

At other moments, the liturgy calls for acclamations: "It is of their nature that they be rhythmically strong, melodically appealing, and affirmative" (*Music in Catholic Worship,* 53). At Mass, the ritual calls for acclamations before the gospel reading and several times within the eucharistic prayer. Acclamations are a form of song for which no book is needed. They are to be known "by heart," by the heart. They have crucial work to do in the most expressive moments of our prayer. An assembly needs a repertoire of these acclamations. They cannot be recited: That would be a contradiction in terms. Singing is the only possibility, and the music must be good enough to become stronger with repetition as the acclamations are used many times each year, over the years. The function of acclamations in prayer is obscured if it is necessary to announce them. The intonation by the cantor or a few notes of instrumental introduction are sufficient to draw everyone present, all ministers included, into singing the acclamations with strength.

There are moments in liturgy where the prayer needs music that is a strong phrase, repeated over and over. This is a litany, a prayer that builds through repetition. It is a form of prayer that the church has used often and well, as in the chanting of the litany of the saints. We use litanies also in the prayers of intercession, some forms of the penitential rite and the Lamb of God.

Litanies are prayers that work in the rhythm of listening and responding. Litanies are most effective when the participants do not need to follow along in a book or song sheet. As in all the kinds of music we have discussed so far in this unit, litanies work best when participants' eyes and hands are free of the printed page. Like acclamations and refrains, litanies do not do their work at the intellectual level alone; their work goes further than merely taking in and reflecting on the meaning of the words being sung. They work at a far deeper level, where the rhythms of the singing create a prayer that echoes in the whole person. That is what music is meant to do in liturgy.

Another familiar form of music that suits certain moments in the liturgy is the hymn. When we sing hymns, we usually need a book or song sheet. Hymns are best suited to the moments that prepare for and conclude the liturgy: They can invite us into our prayer together and can provide grand moments of conclusion for the prayer.

The forest is as important as the trees: How does all the music work together, make the liturgy musical, give shape and tone to the entire service? Very different styles of music may often work well together within a liturgy, even contributing to this integrity.

The liturgical judgment of "what kind of music is called for" is also about the seasons, about the way that musicians and liturgy planners listen to, reflect upon and identify the sounds of Advent or Lent; about the rhythms, instruments and moods that exemplify the seasons. With consistency within each season from year to year, familiar sounds make us feel at home in our church.

1. Some assemblies sing with strength, but some assemblies just don't sing at all. They seem to be too bored or irritated to sing. They probably have good reasons! Maybe all the hymns sound the same. Maybe nobody ever taught them the hymns or acclamations properly. Maybe they are asked to sing the same hymns too often, or maybe they never hear the same hymn twice. Sometimes an assembly won't sing because the text is too small to read, or because the hymn is too hard to sing. Or because the ministers don't sing. Or because no one leads. Or because the leader makes the hymn into a showcase for solo song stylist. In some places the acoustics are so bad that no one can hear anyone else singing. In some places the organist never plays the same thing the same way twice, and no one knows which way the rhythm or melody will go. In your community, what energizes congregational singing? What hinders it?

2. Make a list of your community's repertoire. Include hymns, acclamations, psalms and litanies. Divide the selections by their use in liturgy and by the seasons of the year. Are there particular areas where the assembly sings with strength and confidence? Are there particular areas where they do not?

3. If any areas are weak, the problem might be the quality of the current selections. Would a year-long program for improving (not just increasing) the repertoire be helpful?

Music has been a unique means of celebrating . . .

[the] richness and diversity [of the paschal

mystery] and of communicating the rhythm of the church

year to the assembly. Music enhances the power

of the readings and prayer to capture

the special quality of the liturgical seasons. . . .

Great care must be shown in the selection of music for

seasons and feasts. Contemporary culture seems

increasingly unwilling either to prepare

for or to prolong Christian feasts and seasons.

The Church's pastors and ministers must be aware

of cultural phenomena which run counter to

the liturgical year or even devalue our feasts and

seasons, especially through consumerism.

Liturgical Music Today, *47–48*

Environment: 1
People and Places

hen we meet to pray, we meet somewhere. It's that simple. That somewhere, some place, some space is the environment of prayer. What is that space? How does it best serve the prayer that is done there? How do we shape our spaces and how do they shape us?

A beginning point as we think about this environment question might be the word "church." Christians in the first centuries would not have understood expressions like "I'll meet you in front of the church," or "We're going to renovate the church," or "Is this church fireproof?" The building where the early Christians met to pray was called the *domus ecclesiae,* "the house of the church." The church was the assembly, the people, the faithful; the building had a different name. The question of whether their terminology would work for us is not as important as what their terminology tells us about their thinking: The first consideration was the people. A place for the people to gather could always be found.

This primacy of people was re-emphasized by the 1978 statement of the Bishops' Committee on the Liturgy, *Environment and Art in Catholic Worship.* "To speak of environmental and artistic requirements of Catholic worship, we have to begin with ourselves—we who are the Church, the baptized, the initiated." (27) Begin with ourselves: Who we are, what we are like, what our needs for prayer are, what we would find to be a true home for ourselves, a house in which we can pray. "Among the symbols with which liturgy deals, none is more important than this assembly of believers." (28)

Nothing about the space where we gather is to overshadow us when we are praying. "The most powerful experience of the sacred is found in the action of the assembly: the living words, the living gestures, the living sacrifice, the living meal. This was at the heart of the earliest liturgies. Early church architectural floor plans give evidence of places designed as general gathering spaces, spaces which allowed the whole assembly to be part of the action." (29)

Every consideration about the space (whether it is new or old) and the objects in it grows from this feeling that liturgy is the work of this assembled people, this church. What will help these people pray as a people? What will

nurture the very best that each person is capable of and counter the culture's low estimate of our human capacity for beauty and for sharing? What will keep us from thinking about the assembly as an audience, or as so many individuals praying? What will keep alive in us "concerns for feelings of conversion, support, joy, repentance, trust, love, memory, movement, gesture, wonder" (35)?

What do we know about rooms that show a deep respect for the people who occupy them? Think of the various spaces that we know: theaters, stores, schools, offices, libraries, hospitals, prisons, factories, homes. One quality that is part of this respect could be called hospitality. Obviously, such a quality cannot be separated from hospitable people—yet there is something in a physical environment that may invite or may discourage this, something that makes it easier or harder for us to feel welcome, comfortable, at home. We know this quality when we meet it or miss it in a neighbor's home or a doctor's office. It is not as simple as the color of the walls or the fabric of the curtains, or the carpet being clean or dirty. These things contribute something to how the space makes us feel, but hospitality is about how they all come together, about what they as a whole do to us, and about the way the building gathers us together helps us to remember, acknowledge and celebrate our Christian identity.

Certainly one part of this experience of hospitality is beauty. A space that is beautiful, objects that are beautiful elevate the human spirit; they welcome us and welcome our prayer. Another part of this experience is simplicity: Without this, a space could not witness to the gospel that we accept; without this, a space would not welcome Christian prayer. These two things, beauty and simplicity, can sometimes be in tension. But a space that is hospitable, that reflects and helps create the spirit of the people who gather there, is a place where such tensions are gradually resolved.

Finally, a truly hospitable environment "disappears" in the hospitality of the people. A hospitable space leads toward, fosters, never stands in the way of people's actions. "As common prayer and ecclesial experience, liturgy flourishes in a climate of hospitality: a situation in which people are comfortable with one another, either knowing or being introduced to one another; a space in which people are seated together, with mobility, in view of one another as well as the focal points of the rite, involved as participants and not as spectators." (11)

1. What effect does environment have on your daily attitudes? Compare the environments of different homes, grocery stores, libraries and the like. How does the environment work for or against what is supposed to happen in the place? Do the people there reflect or contribute to the environment? How?

2. The renewal of the liturgy calls for renewal in the place where we pray—a renewal that is more than just changing the sanctuary furniture. The participation of the assembly, the variety of ministries and the ritual itself suggest the reshaping of the whole space. Search out places that are noted for good liturgical space, new or renovated. Discuss the worship area in light of the bishops' statement on environment and art.

3. List the actions that happen in the liturgy, including the actions of the assembly. Does the space help the actions? How? Does it hinder any actions? How?

Let us build a house where love can dwell

And all can safely live,

A place where saints and children tell

How hearts learn to forgive.

Built of hopes and dreams and visions,

Rock of faith and vault of grace;

Here the love of Christ shall end divisions:

All are welcome, all are welcome,

All are welcome in this place.

Let us build a house where love is found

In water, wine and wheat:

A banquet hall on holy ground,

Where peace and justice meet.

Here the love of God, through Jesus,

Is revealed in time and space;

As we share in Christ the feast that frees us:

All are welcome, all are welcome,

All are welcome in this place.

Let us build a house where hands will reach

Beyond the wood and stone

To heal and strengthen, serve and teach,

And live the word they've known.

Here the outcast and the stranger

Bear the image of God's face;

Let us bring an end to fear and danger:

All are welcome, all are welcome,

All are welcome in this place.

Marty Haugen

Environment: 2
Quality and Appropriateness

wareness and acceptance of our prayer as something for the whole person—body, mind, senses, imagination, emotions, memory—has been the constant glory of our Catholic prayer. We maintain that the eating and drinking has to happen, the water has to flow, the scripture has to be told. We put a good cloth on the altar table, light the candles, kiss the cross, burn the incense, lay on the hands. Yet, as *Environment and Art in Catholic Worship* acknowledges, we sometimes let our symbols fade into mere accessories, we sometimes try to make them manageable and efficient.

We hold up certain criteria for the arts with which we form our prayer. Two of these demands that liturgy makes on the arts are named in this document: quality and appropriateness. These apply to music, to the spoken word, to movement. Let us consider these two criteria in relation to the environment, and specifically to the objects we use in our prayer.

"Quality is perceived only by contemplation, by standing back from things and really trying to see them, trying to let them speak to the beholder.... Quality means love and care in the making of something, honesty and genuineness with any materials used, and the artist's special gift in producing a harmonious whole, a well-crafted work." (20) What does that mean when we take it off the page and into our church buildings? Look at the Easter candle by the font. Is it honest? Is it genuine? Well-crafted? Does it appear that love and care were in the making of it? Stand back and contemplate that candle. It says a lot to you, doesn't it? What does it say? That is the point: Things speak to us. Sometimes we try to say with mere words what things can say more clearly and deeply for themselves. An object made with quality leads us into contemplation and—lo and behold!—the object is a work of art that speaks for itself.

An object of quality says something about what we mean. That is what happens with liturgy. The bread and wine, the water of baptism, the oil of the sick: We need not tell each other in words what these things mean. Rather, in the sharing of bread and wine, in the washing with water, in the anointing with oil, we learn what we mean. To muffle the speech of these symbols is to muffle our own selves.

The second criterion is appropriateness. That means that the work of art "must be capable of bearing the weight of mystery, awe, reverence, and wonder which the liturgical action expresses" (21). Good liturgy is content with honest things, as beautiful and simple as they can be. "Bearing the weight" is exactly what appropriate liturgical objects do. The plastic candle, the banner that carries only a slogan, the wafers that bear no resemblance to real bread—these sag under the weight of mystery, of wonder. What could bear that weight but honest things, things that are what they appear to be, and so awaken awe and reverence for what is? The building, the book of scriptures, all the objects we use in liturgy are appropriate when they can bear the weight of mystery "so that we see and experience both the work of art and something beyond it" (22).

Something is appropriate when it serves the liturgy. Is the shape of the room at the service of the assembly's prayer? Does the lighting in the room enhance the prayer? Is the room hospitable, welcoming, human, warm? Do the acoustics of the room help our sung liturgy and proclamation of the word? These are some of the questions that can help us determine what is appropriate for liturgy.

The church needs to support the work of those who have the gifts and the training to bring quality and appropriateness to every object used in the liturgy. The bishops' statement notes: "A major and continuing educational effort is required among believers in order to restore respect for competence and expertise in all the arts and a desire for their best use in public worship. This means winning back to the service of the Church professional people whose places have long since been taken by 'commercial' producers, or volunteers who do not have the appropriate qualifications. Both sensitivity to the arts and willingness to budget resources for these are the conditions of progress so that quality and appropriateness can be real." (26)

1. What is your favorite room? What makes it your favorite: its beauty, size, shape, color, other things? Is it only these, or is it also the people you have shared the room with that make you love it?

2. In your community, how does the shape of the room serve the assembly's prayer and song? Is the room hospitable, welcoming, human, warm?

3. How are the acoustics? Do they enliven the community's worship, or muffle it?

4. What effect do different flooring surfaces have on communal prayer? Visit a parish that has a carpeted floor in its worship space and think about how it sounds. Visit a parish with a hardwood, terrazzo, tile or stone floor in its worship space and think about how it sounds. Discuss the differences in light of "quality and appropriateness" in serving the liturgy.

To be true to itself and to protect its own integrity, liturgy must make demands. Basically, its demands are two: *quality* and *appropriateness*. Whatever the style or type, no art has a right to a place in liturgical celebration if it is not of high quality and if it is not appropriate (GIRM, 254).

Quality is perceived only by contemplation, by standing back from things and really trying to *see* them, trying to let them speak to the beholder. Cultural habit has conditioned the contemporary person to look at things in a more pragmatic way: "What is it worth?" "What will it do?" Contemplation sees the hand stamp of the artist, the honesty and care that went into an object's making, the pleasing form and color and texture. Quality means love and care in the making of something, honesty and genuineness with any materials used, and the artist's special gift in producing a harmonious whole, a well-crafted work. . . .

Appropriateness is another demand that liturgy rightfully makes upon any art that would serve its action. The work of art must be appropriate in two ways: 1) it must be capable of bearing the weight of mystery, awe, reverence, and wonder which the liturgical action expresses; 2) it must clearly *serve* (and not interrupt) ritual action which has its own structure, rhythm and movement.

Environment and Art in Catholic Worship, *19–21*

Environment: 3
Some Specifics

ome aspects of the worship space have more effect on the community's prayer than others. Most of the quotations in this article are from *Environment and Art in Catholic Worship.*

1. *Seating.* In many churches, the seating in the worship space follows the philosophy of theaters, where the main idea is that people need to see the place where things are happening. But at liturgy, while this is important, it is also important that people see each other's faces, not just the backs of heads, that no one feel removed from what is being done (for we are all doing it together), and that there be some freedom of movement. In their document, the bishops speak of "benches or chairs," rather than pews, and these benches or chairs "should be so constructed and arranged that they maximize feelings of community and involvement.... This means striving for a seating pattern and furniture that do not constrict people, but encourage them to move about when it is appropriate" (68). The chairs used by the presider and other ministers "should be so constructed and arranged that they too are clearly part of the one assembly, yet conveniently situated for the exercise of their respective offices" (70).

2. *Altar.* "The altar, the holy table, should be the most noble, the most beautifully designed and constructed table the community can provide. It is the common table of the assembly, a symbol of the Lord, at which the presiding minister stands and upon which are placed the bread and wine and their vessels and the book." (71) The document suggests that the "holy table...should not be elongated, but square or slightly rectangular" (72). A cloth of good quality in design, texture and color may be placed on the table to cover it, but other things—candles, cross, flowers—are placed elsewhere (95, 72).

3. *Font.* The *Rite of Christian Initiation of Adults* reminds us that immersion as a mode of baptism most clearly symbolizes our participation in the death and resurrection of Christ (RCIA, 22). The *National Statutes for the Catechumenate,* which appear at the end of the *Rite of*

Christian Initiation of Adults ritual book, states: "Baptism by immersion is the fuller and more expressive sign of the sacrament and, therefore, preferred" (17). Logically, this requires that the font be large enough for an adult to be immersed in it.

4. *Books.* "Any book which is used by an officiating minister in a liturgical celebration should be of a large (public, noble) size, good paper, strong design, handsome typography and binding.... The use of pamphlets and leaflets detracts from the visual integrity of the total liturgical action." (91)

Let us consider the assembly's worship aids in view of what has been said about hospitality, quality and appropriateness in liturgy. Do inexpensive monthly booklets, usually worn and tattered after only a few uses, speak of hospitality and welcome, dignity and joy, of respect for the ministry of the assembly? Or do they speak of cheapness and unimportance? Are "the hand stamp of the artist, the honesty and care...the pleasing form" that go into quality evident in the worship aids? Are they appropriate to the noble simplicity of the liturgy?

5. *Bread.* The pope and the bishops together in council established that the bread used in the liturgy is to "appear as actual food," and that it "be made in such a way that the priest can break it and distribute the parts to at least some of the faithful" (*General Instruction of the Roman Missal,* 282–283). Recipes for unleavened bread made from wheat flour are available; they yield a bread that looks and tastes and smells like real food.

6. *Tabernacle.* The church reserves the eucharistic bread "to bring communion to the sick and to be the object of private devotion." The tabernacle is to be in a "room or chapel specifically designed and separate from the major space... so that no confusion can take place between the celebration of the eucharist and reservation" (78). This chapel serves the community's prayer best when it offers easy access and "support[s] private meditation without distractions" (79).

1. The material elements used in worship can greatly enhance a celebration. A fine altar cloth, a handsome set of cruets, well-made vestments add a great deal to the character of worship. Objects of less quality or appropriateness can weaken what otherwise what would speak powerfully to us. List some of the material elements used at worship. Think of the purpose each has. In your parish, how are the judgments of quality and appropriateness applied?

2. Examine each of these elements in your building in the light of the questions listed below:

   a. paschal candle; eucharistic bread; incense; seating; musical instruments; statuary and iconography; ambo; altar; font; participation aid.

   b. Who uses this object? How does it help the liturgical action? Is this a full, clear symbol (as opposed to a minimum requirement)? If any object is less appropriate than others, can it be made better? How?

3. Think of the items that are changed to meet the requirements of the changing liturgical seasons. Do they coordinate? Do they meet the criteria of appropriateness and quality in every season?

As a sparrow homing,

a swallow seeking a nest

to hatch its young,

I am eager for your altars,

Lord of heaven's might,

my king, my God.

Psalm 84

Christians have not hesitated to use every human art in their celebration of the saving work of God in Jesus Christ, although in every historical period they have been influenced, at times inhibited, by cultural circumstances. In the resurrection of the Lord, all things are made new. Wholeness and healthiness are restored, because the reign of sin and death is conquered. Human limits are still real and we must be conscious of them. But we must also praise God and give God thanks with the human means we have available. God does not need liturgy; people do, and people have only their own arts and styles of expression with which to celebrate.

Environment and Art in Catholic Worship, 4

Knowing What It Feels Like

e have discussed some of the various elements that are important in our rituals under the headings of Word, Movement, Music and Environment. These are simple things; this is why we can use them in so many different ways. They are human activities, human arts, that can transcend their practical purposes of communicating information, moving the body from place to place and so on to open us to our own spirit and all the mystery of existence.

The history of any group of believers, Jews and Christians included, shows that over the generations, rituals change and evolve. The ways in which word, movement, music and environment come together are adjusted over time to express more clearly the people's faith as it grows and changes over the centuries. Rituals are not formulated from a people's theology, as if some scholar sat down and thought: Because we believe this and that about God and this and that about ourselves, therefore our ritual will do this, and then that, and so on. No, rituals spring naturally from the faith, from the spirit: The spirit of gratitude leads to the lifting up of hands in the first morning light, the spirit of sorrow leads to ashes rubbed on the face. Words, sounds, music, gestures, objects—these are the stuff by which ritual takes shape and lives within the community. This is how a community tells what its life means, and this in turn strengthens that meaning.

Ritual is closely associated with repetition. A people gives ritual expression to their beliefs around things that occur over and over. Among some peoples, these things include the coming of the rainy season, or the gathering of the harvest, or the full moon. There are also rituals that mark off time, like the modern urban rites of TGIF (Thank God It's Friday). And there are daily rituals of meals, of morning, of evening and night. A people has rituals around the great events of life: birth, growing to adulthood, marriage, death. Rituals allow the heart of the matter to take expression in this particular moment, this particular situation.

The repetition of rituals, some yearly, some every few days, some once in a lifetime, some every day, brings a great deal of definition to how the various elements of a ritual take shape. We have dinner every evening, but not like Thanksgiving dinner. We don't greet our spouse on the morning of our wedding anniversary the same way we do every other morning. The rituals of every day are structured simply, with freedom for them to take on some of each day's uniqueness. The less frequently observed rituals are often structured more elaborately.

When we look at Sunday eucharist or the celebrations of baptism or funerals in a parish setting, or look at the ways a family's morning prayer or meal prayer might be done, we know that the ways word and movement and music and environment come together in any ritual depend somewhat on the frequency of that ritual. When we view all the ways ritual works in a parish, we know that our tradition gives us a great number of ways to pray, some meant for every day, some for once a year and some for once a lifetime. What each ritual in a parish is like depends very much on the wise use of the riches of our tradition. If, for example, the only ritual a community experiences is the Sunday eucharist, it would be difficult for the members of that community to nourish a full life of faith, for they would be lacking a great part of our ritual heritage.

We can best help our liturgy to be the work of the people in all its fullness when we are aware of how ritual works and what our heritage contributes. We need strong and simple rituals, mainly the Sunday eucharist, that echo with the mood of feasts and seasons and ordinary times. Within each Mass, we need to do our rituals with a dynamic, a rhythm, a flow that allows all of the elements—word, movement, music, environment—to work to the best possible advantage for our common prayer. We also need daily rituals that connect us with one another and with the great faith tradition we share, for which we assemble every Sunday.

1. What are some of the daily, weekly and seasonal rituals of individuals, family or parish by which we express our faith? How do we care for these? How do they care for us?

2. Choose one ritual of those named above. What are its elements? What does this set of elements do for us?

3. How is eucharist an action we do together?

4. What are the most important elements of "doing Sunday eucharist?"

5. What does the faithful "doing of eucharist" do for us?

'Tis the gift to be simple, 'tis the gift to be free,

'tis the gift to come down where we ought to be,

and when we find ourselves in the place just right,

'twill be in the valley of love and delight.

When true simplicity is gained

to bow and to bend we shan't be ashamed,

to turn, turn, will be our delight

till by turning, turning we come round right.

'Tis the gift to be simple, 'tis the gift to be free,

'tis the gift to come down where we ought to be,

and when we find ourselves in the place just right,

'twill be in the valley of love and delight.

Shaker hymn "'Tis the Gift to be Simple"

All Together: 2
Rhythm and Pace

iturgy has its own structure, rhythm and pace: a gathering, a building up, a climax, and a descent to dismissal. It alternates between persons and groups of persons, between sound and silence, speech and song, movement and stillness, proclamation and reflection, word and action." (*Environment and Art in Catholic Worship*, 25) The potential of any liturgical celebration, whether it enhances the ability of the participants to pray fully through this ritual, depends on how well all these rhythms are put to the service of the prayer. From one point of view, a ritual is just a series of elements, like beads on a string: This one comes before that one but after that one. This point of view means that the participants feel no sense of ownership of their liturgy. No, rather than that, we engage in rituals that have been expressive of Christian prayer through the ages and are now entrusted to our hands so that we may pray well and have something to pass on to those who follow.

When we feel that the liturgy is our prayer, the celebration of these people right here in this tradition, then we know that the elements of the liturgy are not beads on a string, but human actions. They are ours. We can reflect upon them. Naming some of the elements in the rhythm of the liturgy, as the document quoted above does, helps this reflection: "It alternates . . . between sound and silence, speech and song, movement and stillness, proclamation and reflection, word and action" (25). Before we discuss these elements by the names we have given them in a particular ritual, whether "gospel," or "acclamation," or "blessing," we can talk about them in terms of the kind of action they are: That is, how do they come about? What makes them happen? How do people react?

Between sound and silence. In some traditions, most ritual prayer is done in silence. Our tradition insists on the importance of silence, even in common prayer, while giving greater prominence to sound (spoken words, sung words, music, bells). But each gains its power from the other. Whenever, for example, the word of God is proclaimed, there is a human need for reflection and silence serves this best. It is possible that the "hurry-up" of modern society has become so natural to us that it is difficult to allow a silence to last longer than a few seconds. But this would throw off the rhythm, the back and forth of sound and silence. For reflection and prayer to flourish, we need the silence to last long enough that we can settle into it. Silent prayer in common, assembly and ministers and presider together, has a quality and a power that is not the same as an individual's silent prayer. The assembly, in this kind of silence, knows what it means to be praying together. The silence allows the words to echo in the assembly's heart. In a similar way, a gifted musician was once asked how he handled the notes so well and answered, "The notes I handle no better than many others, but the rests between the notes—that is where the art resides."

Between speech and song. Some elements of liturgy need the power of song by their very nature, especially acclamations, litanies and psalms. Other elements, because of their importance to the liturgy, should be given special emphasis and reverence: important blessings, the eucharistic prayer. Still other elements, especially the scriptures, usually work best when they are spoken.

Between movement and stillness. Stillness balances the movements of processions and gestures. Stillness is necessary at certain times, and its absence can be conspicuous. Stillness is particularly necessary during silence. If during a silence the minister is looking through the book or cleaning the cups and plates, no matter how discreetly, then the power of the silence and stillness is diminished.

Reverence has everything to do with pace, with timing. When liturgy is the work of the whole person, the spirit and body together, then the beauty of prayer makes for a pace that is reverent. The liturgical way of doing something has nothing to do with efficiency; hurrying liturgy can only seem foolish.

1. Have you ever heard the sound of silence as relatives stand over the crib of the firstborn of a new generation? Or the grand silence of a wave approaching the shore? Or the silence of good friends? Or the expectant silence at an unveiling of art? Silence is the other half of our pulsating life. Listen for it in your prayer.

2. To be silent and still at liturgy is not easy in our noisy, busy culture. But that is all the more reason our silence and stillness at worship is a treasure that keeps the necessary rhythm and pace in the liturgy, that keeps us feeling at home with public prayer. Where in the Mass do we need silence? Are people uneasy at first in a generous period of silence? If so, is there something that can be done about this?

3. What can we do to keep hurriedness out of our liturgy?

4. Notice the differences between a leisurely meal in a comfortable dining room and eating in a fast-food establishment. How do these compare to your experiences of liturgy?

Obedience is a dance learned one step at a time, with faltering step perhaps. The pace may be halting; it is unfamiliar and we are clumsy. Our souls and hearts will be stretched. There will be pain — ask any dancer. But the stretching will leave our souls and hearts with a new breadth, and encompassed in the arms of our Lover God, we will know the freedom of the dance.

Cynthia Stebbins

The primary and exclusive aim of the liturgy is not the expression of the individual's reverence and worship for God. It is not even concerned with the awakening, formation and sanctification of the individual soul as such. Nor does the onus of liturgical action and prayer rest with the individual; it does not even rest with the collective groups, composed of numerous individuals, who periodically achieve a limited and intermittent unity in their capacity as the congregation of the church. The liturgical entity consists rather of the united body of the faithful — the church — a body which infinitely outnumbers the mere congregation. The liturgy is the church's public and lawful act ot worship and it is performed and conducted by the officials whom the church herself has designated for the post — her priests. In the liturgy God is to be honored by the body of the faithful, and the faithful are to derive sanctification from this act of worship. It is important that this objective nature of the liturgy should be fully understood. . . . The fact that the individual Catholic, by his or her absorption into the higher unity, finds unity, finds liberty and discipline, originates in the twofold nature of the human being, who is both social and solitary.

Romano Guardini

All Together: 3
Between Individuals and Groups

he rhythm and the pace that are so important in good liturgy are not just matters of sound and silence, stillness and movement. There are also the rhythms of exchanges between people. This is not an arbitrary arrangement worked out to be sure that everyone has something to do. It is in the nature of liturgy.

In ritual there are different things that need to be done. This in itself sets up a rhythm among the participants, for some will have developed their gifts for leading song, some for reading scripture, some for preaching, some for drawing people together and presiding. All these participants are present first as members of the assembly, and they exercise their various ministries in the service of the whole assembly. The rhythm of the various ritual actions is created as these participants, ministers and assembly, interact. And as ministers develop their gifts for reading, leading song, leading prayer, they also develop their awareness of the ways their ministries support and complement one another.

The *Constitution on the Sacred Liturgy* of Vatican II noted: "In liturgical celebrations each person...who has an office to perform, should do all of, but only, those parts which pertain to that office by the nature of the rite and the principles of liturgy" (28). Certainly there are people who can both read scripture well and lead song well, people who can both play the organ well and preach well. There are even people who can do everything well. But that would not change the principle involved, for it is aimed not only at attaining excellence in each ministry in the liturgy but at this rhythm, this need for many persons to share their gifts, this sense that each person praying needs and deserves many others. The prayer of the community builds as lector, choir, cantor and presider interact with the assembly. And it is interaction: one is not active and the other passive. Passivity discourages good reading, good singing, good presiding, good liturgy. Mutual attention, shown not only in volume of speech or singing but in the eyes and posture, is the greatest spur to presider, cantor and lector and assembly to do their tasks well.

The liturgy of the word offers a good example of this rhythm among persons. A lector proclaims the first scripture reading, and then comes a silence. Out of the silence, a cantor begins to sing the first verse of the psalm and the whole assembly responds with the refrain. A second reading from the scriptures calls for another period of silence. Silence and stillness blossom into the gospel procession as deacon and acolytes move solemnly to the ambo and the whole assembly begins its alleluia acclamation. The gospel is announced and proclaimed and the homily is given. Another silence. Then the presider invites the assembly into prayer and a cantor leads the litany of intercessions.

In each part of the liturgy of the eucharist the dynamic is different. The preparation of the table and gifts has the assembly interacting with those who collect money (or even joining in procession to bring forward money and other gifts for the poor and the church) while some from the assembly bring bread and wine to the table. The presider assists in preparing the table and speaks the prayer that concludes this part of the ritual. In this preparation rite, much depends on how the liturgy is shaped locally. In the eucharistic prayer, the challenge is a strong participation of the assembly as the presider speaks or chants the prayer and everyone present joins in to affirm and acclaim and simply to participate in what is being done. There is a clear conclusion to this in the great Amen. Then the communion rite has a very different rhythm. Here the presider serves to introduce various elements. The presider does this with words for the Lord's Prayer, the peace greeting and the communion procession, and with the action of breaking the bread for the Lamb of God litany. The assembly carries these rites completely: singing the Lord's Prayer, exchanging the peace greeting, singing the Lamb of God litany and making the communion procession. The procession itself has the crucial rhythm between the minister who offers bread or cup and the individual members of the assembly who respond in word and action. Appropriate singing is an essential part of the procession. Afterwards, the silence and stillness should embrace everyone, including all ministers, until the presider concludes the rite with the Prayer after Communion.

In such rhythms the assembly takes its work seriously and the church exercises its tasks in such a way that the Body of Christ is built up.

1. In what other contexts do we experience something like a ritual interaction between "ministers" (who are not called this) and an assembly (who are not called this either)? Think about politics, sports, music, civic, neighborhood and ethnic celebrations.

2. Do the ministers of your community act on cue or are they comfortable with taking responsibility for the rhythm and flow of the liturgy?

3. Do the ministers react smoothly when the unexpected happens (as, because we are human beings, it will)? If not all can, what training would help?

4. How do the ministers make it clear that they are first of all members of the assembly called to serve that assembly?

5. How do the ministers lead by example?

The liturgy not only can but must build on what is suitable in the culture of a people. In our Archdiocese we Catholics come from many cultures with many different gifts. The Lord has brought us all together and we are called to be fully Christ together. In population, we are predominately from Spanish-speaking cultures, with all their own diversity. But we embrace many Asian and Pacific Island cultures as well as the diversity of various African and European cultures that have had their own development on this continent. And there is cultural richness within cultural richness.

This is a difficult challenge. Yes, we want liturgy with sounds and gestures that flow from the religious soul of a people, whether Vietnamese or Mexican, Native American or African American. Yet we have a Catholic soul. We are in need of witnessing to that soul, of being in assemblies where the vision of Paul comes alive, where the Vietnamese, the Mexican, Native American and African American stand side by side around the table singing one thanksgiving to God. And although that thanksgiving may have the rhythm of one particular culture, all will join with their hearts. Before we are anything else — any sex, ethnicity, nationality or citizenship — we need to be the Body of Christ, sisters and brothers by our Baptism. Every one of us needs to know by heart some of the music, vocabulary, movement, and ways of thinking and feeling that are not of our own background. The larger society we are a part of needs this witness.

We have to accomplish two results: to let the prevalent liturgy take on the pace, sounds, and shape that other cultures bring; and to strive in our parishes to witness that in this Church there is finally no longer this people or that people, but one single assembly in Christ Jesus.

Cardinal Roger Mahony

Who Does the Liturgy?

The rituals that shape and change human life and the life of the world happen when people of faith come together. They just don't happen when we are alone. We bring to the rituals what we have: needs and gifts.

In the great rituals of the Christian tradition, especially the eucharist, the various elements—the scriptures to be read, the psalms to be sung, the communion to be shared—call for many gifts from many different people acting together.

Good ritual is not magic; it is not automatic. It needs what all of us together can give to it. Here we look more closely at the various ministers of the assembly who help us do the liturgy of the church.

Who Does the Liturgy?

he words "ministry" and "minister" are heard more and more frequently. We hear, for example, of ministry to the sick, ministers of communion, the ministry of the deacon. These words help us understand how we relate to one another in the church community. Reflection on the scriptures and saints has impressed on us that there are many ministries in the church. And in every case, the one who ministers (to the sick, to those in prison, and so on) is also ministered to.

When we speak of ministry in the liturgy or of the various liturgical ministers such as acolytes and ushers, we express our awareness of how various members of the church take on specific tasks. We also express our awareness that these tasks are in the service of the whole community. As *Environment and Art in Catholic Worship* says: "God does not need liturgy; people do, and people have only their own arts and styles of expression with which to celebrate" (4). In our need for liturgy, for good ritual done together, we offer our skills in this or that art so that the liturgy may be beautiful and strong. This is all that we have. This use of ourselves is ministry. Each minister—usher or cantor or homilist—emerges from the community. It is there in the church itself, that we find what ministry truly means. Ministry is basically the way Christians are, the way they behave. Eugene Walsh has developed this thought:

> We readily make ministry equivalent to "service." Indeed this has been a step forward, but I maintain we must have yet a radically different view of what ministry really is. Henri Nouwen offers the clearest insight into this new view when he insists that to minister does not mean "do things for" people, but rather "to be with" them. To minister, at its deepest level, means "to be present" to others. It means to care for others enough that you are willing to "be with" them, to keep on "paying attention" to them, to keep on staying in attendance to them. Personal presence comes first in effective ministry. If, while you are being present, there are also things to do for people, and services to offer, that is fine. But "doing for" is secondary to the being present.... Being a real minister becomes much more demanding. *(The Ministry of the Celebrating Community)*

This is helpful in understanding what really happens in the liturgy. All of the ministries are certainly about service. But that is true of most human rituals: In order to have a Fourth of July parade or a Thanksgiving dinner many people take on special roles and so serve the larger community. What distinguishes this ministering at liturgy is the minister's motivation: What comes first is not the worthy exercise of one's role, but the fact that through this role one can be present, be there, be with others.

That is not to diminish the importance of doing the ministry well. It is not necessarily true that good will is all that is needed for someone to be capable of any ministry. In fact, each ministry calls for very specific qualities, qualities which in most cases are present and recognizable in a person and are then developed as the person learns and does the specific ministry. Ministries are functions of the rituals we celebrate: They are not offices or ranks around which we make our prayer. Rather, liturgical ministries develop naturally from the common prayer itself as ways to bring about worthy expressions of word, music, movement, environment and the patterns that these take.

As we speak of the various ministries, we naturally have in mind the Mass as our most familiar community ritual. However, ministries are part of every gathering for prayer: morning prayer, the recitation of the rosary, the sacrament of reconciliation. When we look at each rite and ask what it is that we are doing, what kind of prayer we want this to be, we know what the ministries are that bring that about.

No one, of course, can do everything at liturgy equally well. Some people have the qualities that make them truly welcoming ushers, while other qualities make for outstanding lectors and others for inspiring ministers of communion. When people with certain qualities are matched with the liturgical roles that call for those qualities, the ritual can speak most powerfully to us, moving us to prayer. Good ministers breathe fresh life into the rituals that breathe fresh life into all of us.

1. Who does the liturgy in your community?

2. What needs are there in the liturgy — for instance, readings to be proclaimed, environment to be decorated, collection to be taken up, announcements to be made. How are these taken care of? What different qualities in people do these different needs call for?

3. How are the different liturgical ministries coordinated?

The liturgy, then, is rightly seen as an exercise of the priestly office of Jesus Christ. In the liturgy the sanctification of women and men is given expression in symbols perceptible by the senses and is carried out in ways appropriate to each of them. In it, complete and definitive public worship is performed by the mystical body of Jesus Christ, that is, by the Head and his members.

Constitution on the Sacred Liturgy, 7

Because of the central role of liturgical rites in disclosing within a community the important delineations and for presenting the mysterious holiness of God, the liturgical assembly will continue to be, as it has been for centuries, decisive for the church's self-understanding. It is in assembly that what the church knows to be true can and must be celebrated, and the very physical shape this public praise of the holy God takes will contribute to the slower work of theological reflection.

Mary Collins

The Assembly

any things have to be done by many people for the liturgy on Sunday to be celebrated in a parish. There is the priest, who is leader and presider. There is the lector, who prepares and reads the scriptures. There is the leader of song. There is an organist or other musicians. There are those who help with the distribution of holy communion. There are the acolytes or servers. There are the ushers. Perhaps there is a deacon. There is the homilist, usually the presider or the deacon. And, behind the scenes but just as important, there are those who prepared the building by cleaning and decorating, those who wrote special parts of the liturgy for this Sunday and those who helped to coordinate the whole thing. And don't forget those who made the wine and baked the bread.

All these people have a ministry only because of the assembly—that's the name we use for everyone present. All of them are members of the assembly before being lector or usher. And what is the ministry of the assembly?

Think about these other rituals. What would a birthday party be like if no one sang "Happy Birthday"? What would a football game be like if no one cheered? Or what would Christmas dinner be like if no one spoke to anyone else? All these events, these rituals, call for people to do special tasks: cake baking, cheerleading, sparking the conversation. But more than that, before all that, they need people who are eager to lend voices, hands and even hearts to make something happen, people who just want to be together and make their time together a good time.

All the special ministries depend on what we are all a part of: the assembly. That seems to be quite a change from thinking about Sunday Mass as "going to church," or "attending Mass," from thinking about Mass as a time to say private prayers while the priest and servers did the ceremonies of the liturgy. It seems to be quite a change from what people seem to have in mind when they head for the last pew and try not to sit too close to anyone else. All the changes of the last thirty years or so are not for God's sake, they are for the sake of the assembly: to make it possible for us to see our ministry and claim it. Presiders, lectors and musicians can do only so much: The liturgy is done by the assembly. The assembly—we—gather together for the sake of remembering who we are as God's people and in the midst of that realization we offer our praise and thanks and intercession and repentance.

The way this is done is very concrete. The first thing an assembly does is assemble, making one another welcome, taking places near the altar table and near to one another. Assemblies have to assemble, to get together: That is as essential to the ministry of the assembly as a voice is to the ministry of the song leader. The liturgy is not untouched by whether or not we smile at one another, whether or not we sit together, whether or not we pay attention to each other. By such things can our liturgy be made powerful and real or be diminished into abstraction.

This assembling together need not be forced. We do not have to change our personality in order to show our faith. We come together for the praying of the community. It takes nothing away from the beauty of that prayer to be serious enough about it to be familiar with it.

During the liturgy of the word, the assembly's part is listening to the proclamation of the word of God. There is no need for the members of the assembly to use printed texts, except individuals whose language is not the same as that being read aloud, or whose hearing is impaired, or who, for some other reason, are unable to understand the proclamation. The assembly supports the lector and the presider by giving them our eyes, a sign of our full attention, and by making clear, strong responses. During the liturgy of the word, we also reflect on what we have heard in silence and in the psalm refrain. Standing, we join in the strong acclamation for the gospel. We listen to the homilist share reflections on the scriptures. And we join in a litany of intercessions for all the world and the church universal.

During the eucharistic prayer, the assembly's part is acclamation. The acclamations are how we give voice to our praise and thanksgiving (which is what the word "eucharist" means).

Then the bread is broken, and the assembly shares communion. Throughout the liturgy, bodily posture and movement are important parts of the assembly's ministry: At communion, they are vital. In the procession, in the reverence with which we hold the bread and the cup and ourselves, we experience our holy communion with our Lord.

The liturgy asks much of the assembly. Some of what liturgy needs from all of us is to be spoken, some to be sung, some to be communicated by the eyes, some by the whole body, some by our awareness of ourselves as an assembly, not merely as individuals who happen to be in the same place at the same time. The assembly's ministry makes all the difference.

In the early 1900s, as the liturgical movement was gaining momentum, one sentence that summarized the renewal of the liturgy was repeatedly heard: "Pray the Mass." This sounds obvious to us now, but it was the cause of a great deal of discussion and even resistance at the time. "Pray the Mass" pointed toward the assembly's right and privilege to celebrate eucharist actively. For the early liturgical reformers, just as for us today, active participation meant something different than keeping busy with singing and making responses. Active participation means that no one is a spectator. Everyone, by the virtue of baptism, actively offers the one sacrifice of thanksgiving; everyone is a celebrant, with one presider. The shape and quality of worship then does not depend entirely upon the presider, musicians or liturgy planners, but upon every member of the whole assembly. We add ourselves to every act of worship.

1. Have you previously thought that liturgy was for God? Are there practical dimensions to saying: "God does not need liturgy; people do"?

2. What are implications of this chapter for your community?

3. How will you raise the "assembly awareness" of those who always sit in the back of your church?

Among the symbols with which liturgy deals, none is more important than this assembly of believers. It is common to use the same name to speak of the building in which those persons worship, but that is misleading. In the words of ancient Christians, the building used for worship is called *domus ecclesiae,* the house of the church.

The most powerful experience of the sacred is found in the celebration and the persons celebrating, that is, it is found in the action of the assembly: the living words, the living gestures, the living sacrifice, the living meal.

Environment and Art in Catholic Worship, *28–29*

❖

The commitment I envision must be in our Catholic bones: the need to assemble each Sunday, to make common prayer in song, to hear the scriptures and reflect on them, to intercede for all the world, to gather at the holy table and give God thanks and praise over the bread and wine which are for us the body and blood of our Lord Jesus Christ, and finally to go from that room to our separate worlds — but now carrying the tune we have heard, murmuring the words we have made ours, nourished by the sacred banquet, ready in so many ways to make all God's creation and all the work of human hands into the kingdom we have glimpsed in the liturgy.

Cardinal Joseph Bernardin

The Presider

he word "presider" is often used instead of "celebrant" to designate the person who leads the assembly in worship. It is a more precise word because everyone present actually celebrates the liturgy, but only one person serves as presider. The word does have its drawbacks: It is associated with presiding at meetings, or judges presiding in courtrooms. But the word does point to what is most basic in this ministry: The priest-celebrant serves as a focus for the community's prayer. He knows the liturgy thoroughly and is completely at home with its rhythms—not so that he can act as a master of ceremonies, but to lend the assembly confidence and inspiration and lead the common prayer. The presider serves the assembly in the way he does the greeting, keeps the silences, listens to the scriptures, leads the prayers.

Until Vatican II's reform of the liturgy, the presider typically handled the work of several ministries. He had the deacon's ministry, the lector's, and sometimes a few others. Now we know which tasks and skills belong to the presider and which belong to other ministers. Basically, the presider's ministry includes some spoken parts: greeting the assembly and calling them to prayer in the introductory rites; introducing and concluding the petitions; leading the eucharistic prayer; leading the prayer after communion and blessing the assembly. The gospel proclamation and various invitations belong to the deacon, and the homily may be preached by the deacon.

The spoken words belonging to the presider are few, but this indicates their importance. If the presider were to take on other roles, or add commentary at various points, then the important parts proper to only him would begin to appear trivial. Presiding includes more than just spoken parts alone: The lifting of the hands in prayer, the breaking of the bread and sharing of communion, for example, are vital elements of the presider's role.

The qualities that make for a good presider include the following:

Awareness that he is a member of the assembly. The presider belongs as everyone else there belongs, a baptized Christian come to praise and thank the Lord. This is clear in small ways and large: He sings when the assembly sings, in hymns, acclamations and refrains; he listens when the assembly listens and keeps silent reflection with the assembly; his manner is that of a friend. The presider is not "the star of the show" but the one who helps us all focus on who we are and what we are really doing.

Grace in movement, reverence in gesture. The manner matters. What one does with hands and eyes and the whole body communicates presence and attitude. If a presider were to say, "The grace and peace of our Lord Jesus Christ be with you," but his eyes were not on the assembly, his arms not open in greeting, then he would not be presiding. If a presider were to say, "Lift up your hearts," while turning pages in the book, then no hearts would be lifted. If he were to handle the bread and wine mechanically at the table and at communion, then all the words in the world would not be able to draw us fully into the mystery that is present. No movement of the presider is meaningless: How he sits, walks, extends the peace, blesses, offers communion—all these can add to the community's prayer. Grace in movement and reverence in touch are not "put on" just for the liturgy: They are honest reflections of a person's life, of a person's awareness of the presence of God in all creation.

A prayerful voice. Grace and reverence are found here also, in the tone, volume, pace and cadences of speech. Much of the presider's spoken part, especially in the eucharistic prayers, is made up of familiar words. The presider's challenge is not to make them sound new each time somehow, but rather to speak in a way that fits this occasion of great thanksgiving, that catches the mood of the prayer in its very sound. This is why chanting the prayer texts can be very effective.

A sense of pace. Timing can be everything—not because liturgy is entertainment, but because it is human. Why is the same story moving when one person tells it but dull when another tells it? A sense of pace is something some people just have and that others work hard to attain. At prayer, a sense of pace means a feeling, a sensitivity, for the involvement of the community: knowing the right moment to begin and to end each element of the ritual.

In everything, the assembly supports the presider: through our attention in posture and eyes, through our reverence in gesture, through our strong speech.

The one who is probably most aware of and sensitive to the assembly's ministry is the presider. Presiders often remark that every Mass congregation has its own personality. Some congregations are always responsive, inspiring the presider to more responsiveness in turn. At some Masses the congregation is so subdued that the presider feels alone at worship and consequently finds it difficult to be a spirited presider.

(In this article and the next the masculine pronoun is used because in the Roman Catholic church, priests and deacons are male. All that has been said about the ministry of the presider is equally applicable to ministers who preside at liturgies other than the eucharist, such as the Liturgy of the Hours, communion services or devotions, where the presider may be male or female, ordained or lay.)

1. At one time or another, each of us serves as a presider. This might be at a family meal, a Thanksgiving dinner, class reunion, or other occasion. What does it feel like? What qualities does it call forth?

2. Think of the ministry of the presider in your community. What are some particularly strong points you have observed? Are there any weak points?

3. If there are some weak points, what can you do to help? What are some encouraging ways to invite more effective presiding?

Presiding is a service required by any group of people who have gathered for a common purpose. When that purpose is common prayer in the tradition of people of biblical faith, that meeting is a liturgy. Presiding is, therefore, a service which liturgy requires.

The term "presider" is accurate, even though it needs in any given time and place considerable elaboration. It is accurate because it states clearly and unequivocally a function which must be exercised by someone in a liturgical assembly. It is also theologically sound, because it depends on a gathering, an assembly of God's people, the church. No one is born a presider. No one is made a presider by training or talent or will or desire or anything but the choice and vocation and delegation of the faith community. There are certainly native aptitudes and basic training, but presiders, like all other ministers, are made by the church.

Robert Hovda

The Deacon

he ministry of deacon within the church is not limited to the liturgy. Permanent deacons are involved in every aspect of the church's work and presence. Since liturgy is not just another field of church work, but is where the church is entirely itself, at home, expressing its whole life, deacons have a particular role in the worship service.

The deacon is the one who is responsible for the order of the service. This is seen in the deacon's invitations to the assembly in the peace greeting, the acclamations, the dismissal. This is also clear in the deacon's place beside the presider. If there is no deacon present, the presider makes most of these invitations, and the acolytes can be responsible for the flow of the liturgy. But presider and acolytes do these things not as parts of their own ministry, but as necessary in the absence of the deacon.

One quality necessary in a deacon, then, would be a sense of the dynamics of the ritual, for the ordering of words and movements and music in good strong prayer. The deacon speaks simply and honestly to the assembly; the deacon's hospitality takes shape in the few but warm words of invitation addressed directly to the people.

The deacon reads the gospel. Deacons need to have the skills of a lector and the presence that makes the procession with the book to the ambo a physical announcement and acclamation of the good news.

The deacon addresses the assembly in the prayers of intercession. The deacon's words are invitations: "In peace, let us pray to the Lord." The assembly's response makes the intercessions into prayer: "Lord, hear our prayer," or "Lord, have mercy." The deacon's part is also to lead this litany with strong, clear song, but often, the cantor serves in this role.

The formulating of the petitions may also be part of the deacon's work, since their ministry brings them into close touch with the needs of the whole church, the society, the poor and especially the local community. A parish poet may assist the deacon in phrasing the petitions to inspire prayer.

Frequently, the deacon's liturgical ministry will involve carrying and handling various objects: the thurible when incense is used, the wine vessels, the communion plate and the bread, the gospel book. Reverence and a sense of pace are essential in these movements. The deacon's whole manner must make it clear that it really matters that there is a book, that there is the fragrant incense, that there is bread and wine.

The deacon may preside at Morning or Evening Prayer, at holy communion outside of Mass, at weddings and funerals, at various devotions. The deacons of a community demonstrate that leading public prayer is learned in smaller gatherings, in the prayer of the household, in personal prayer. In this, as in their whole ministry, they make it clear that clergy and laity are not in opposition, that we are all, lay and ordained, in service of all.

Deacons, whose role was re-established by the Second Vatican Council, are not yet part of every community. Their ministry is still developing. Their role is rooted in service and their ministry at the altar is a reflection of that service. This is evident in the deacon's manner in all the liturgical actions: never dominating, never overshadowing the presider or the other ministers.

By service in community, the deacon is instrumental in developing a profound liturgical spirit. The deacon's love of the word of God and ability to show others how to pray are examples of this ministry.

1. Have you seen people take a role like the deacon's in other human communities? Think of school organizations, arts and recreation programs, political and civic groups. When have you seen the role of the deacon handled particularly well in a non-church setting? What made that work so well?

2. In light of the above, is there any area in which your parish's deacons need to develop their skills? If so, how can you help them?

3. Would it be useful for the deacons to share in the planning for liturgy? In what way?

Yours is a share
in the work of the Lord's Spirit
who calls the whole church
to the *diakonia* of the liturgy,
of the word and of charity.

Yours is the task
of preparing the Lord's table
for the prayer of the assembly,
for the communion
of God's people.

Yours is the work of proclaiming the gospel
and preaching it
in season and out of season,
announcing the word of challenge and comfort
that all need to hear.

Yours is the ministry of charity
to those who are in need,
especially Christ's beloved,
the poorest of the poor.

Your hands guide the newly baptized
through the dying and rising of Christ
in the saving waters of the pool and font.

You stand as witness for the church
as a man and woman
bind their lives together
in Christ,
in love,
in fidelity,
in marriage.

Austin Fleming

The Homilist

n many of our liturgies, and especially at the eucharist, we have the tradition of public reflection on the scriptures that have been read. This homily is usually the task of the presider, sometimes of the deacon. The preparation involves at least "…prayer, the scripture study, the familiarity with the life of the community, and the skill of writing or outlining for oral discourse" (Robert Hovda, *Strong, Loving and Wise*).

Those requirements take time and energy. They lead toward a very special way of speaking, a way that is deeply rooted in Jewish and Christian worship. The homily is not simply an explanation of the scriptures, the fruit of research into the best scholarship. Nor is it the drawing of a moral from the scriptures, nor using the scriptures to back up the latest need for school support or abortion law reform. Nor is the homily a great literary creation "from nothing": The scriptures and eucharist are its beginning and its ending. The homilist helps the assembly appreciate the wonderful web that links word and sacrament and daily living.

The homilist reflects on the scriptures, stands before the scriptures. This requires knowledge of the books, the authors, the times, the way they have been used by the church. But all that only clears the way for the homily to take shape. The homilist is not primarily one who interprets the scriptures, but one who is interpreted by them, who can put life and struggle and joy before these texts and share what takes shape. For most homilists, that is hard work. But it is only the beginning—for the homilist must make the work interesting.

How to do that? The first requirement for preaching interestingly is not to use too many words to say things that are simple. This is not a matter of the length of time spent in speaking. A long homily can be interesting, the short homily dull. It is a matter of how explicit, how wordy we are in getting a thing said.

When we examine the teachings of Jesus, we see how economical he was with words. There are some wordy allegorical explanations appended to some of the parables, and scholars have determined that these were not Jesus'

original words, but were added by the evangelists. They are less effective teachers than he. In their attempts to make everything perfectly clear, they multiply words in a dull and foggy way, draining their readers' interest.

This tells us that a preacher must be restrained and not say too much. The homilist has to know not just where to stop altogether, but where to stop in individual sentences. Quality delivery is as important as the product—as any pizza place knows!

> Our Lord's genius in presenting an idea—let's say the idea of compassion—is that he went at it from many different angles. He would make a short thrust, an allusion, then back away. He would tell a story about a compassionate act, and leave it there. The story did the job for him; he never moralized. In five, eight, ten ways he would tease his listeners into reflecting on what it meant to be compassionate. The one thing you can't accuse Jesus of is beating an idea to death.
>
> He was uncanny at appealing to people's experience. They knew how commercial dealing was carried on. They knew it was full of crookedness and self-interest. He didn't linger on that, stopping to deplore it at great length. He just drew on it as an example of the way things were, to move on to deeper matters. If just one listener decided to turn his or her value system around, specific abuses in the world of business or trade would be tackled soon enough. Jesus was never painfully obvious in his teaching. He went to the ethical jugular every time: that basic self-interest that makes living for others an impossibility, unless there is radical change. (Gerard Sloyan in *Liturgy*, May 1974)

The homilist's ministry begins in being a person of prayer in this community, in knowing the people and their concerns. The assembly in turn supports the homilist by giving attention, by serious reflection on what is said, by thoughtful criticism.

1. The role of homilist is probably the most difficult liturgical ministry. In addition to the basic training needed, the homilist also needs to prepare for every homily. This preparation takes a great deal of time, prayer and sensitivity to the assembly. The homilist's work can be enriched through preaching workshops, prayer, scripture study and awareness of world events and local stories to use as meaningful examples. The assembly can be a great source of help to the homilist by expressing spiritual needs clearly and offering feedback in helpful ways. There are many ways to organize this back-and-forth between assembly and homilist. What works best in your community?

2. What makes a good homily good? What makes a poor homily poor?

3. Would it make a difference to omit the Sunday homily?

4. How might a liturgy team and homilist work together on a regular basis?

5. For homilists: In one or two sentences, what are the main points that you want the assembly to take home with them?

Liturgy understood as the worship of the church and social action understood as the work of the church are part, one of the other. Liturgy which does not move its participants to social action is mere ceremonialism; social action which does not find its source in the liturgy is mere humanitarianism.

Cardinal Richard Cushing

The homily is the assembly's conversation with the day's scripture readings. Only by respecting both scripture and the community can the homilist speak for and to the assembly, bringing it together in this time and place with this Sunday's scriptures. Good homilists must be familiar with the community's needs, pains and hopes. They must challenge and encourage. And they must seek out and listen to parishioners' comments. Those who preach should make frequent use of seminars and classes on homiletics and scripture.

Cardinal Joseph Bernardin

The Minister of Music

everal ministries in the liturgy have to do with music: organists and other instrumentalists, choir directors and members, cantors and leaders of song, members of small ensembles of varying styles and combinations of instruments. By this time the classification "folk group" has passed from our vocabulary as musicians have integrated a wide variety of music into the church's repertoire. The development of all these ministries of music witnesses to our awareness that good liturgy is musical liturgy — musical because that is the only way that such essential rites as the acclamations and litanies can be done by the assembly, and musical because the ministries of instrumentalists and choirs not only support the assembly's prayer but greatly enhance processions, times of reflection and much more.

As parishes have grown in their awareness and appreciation of what music can be in the liturgy, they have been inclined to coordinate all the parish musicians through a minister of music. The title may vary, but the job description includes the following elements: directing the choir, training cantors and leaders of song, coordinating music with the planning of the parish liturgy committee. The goal of this work is the musical liturgy of a singing assembly.

The minister of music is also charged with cultivating others' musical skills to contribute to the liturgy. Because of this, a minister may have a solid background in music and music education, but may have not yet had the opportunity to develop as solid a sense for the liturgy. This may be acquired gradually through reading, workshops, summer institutes, experiences of good musical liturgy in other parishes as well as through the informal teaching of the liturgy committee.

In addition, the minister of music works closely with other musicians and with musical groups. The criterion for all their work is quality in any style in order to serve the prayer of the people. The minister's knowledge and imagination will serve to integrate all the musicians' abilities.

The minister of music works closely with and facilitates the training of all those involved in liturgical roles, especially the cantors, leaders of song, organists, choir members, members of small ensembles and the presider, who may sometimes need encouragement to sing or help in preparing.

Cantor. This minister sings the verses of psalms and sometimes of other songs. The assembly sings the refrains. The cantor needs musical abilities and a good sense of the way we pray through music. The cantor's singing is very much like the presider's leading of prayer: The cantor needs to enter into the psalms as prayers just as the presider enters the eucharistic prayer. What the cantor does is prayer.

Leader of song. This is often the same person as the cantor. The leader of song assists the assembly with their hymns and acclamations. This minister works most closely with the main instrumentalist. The leader of song develops a clear sense of when the assembly's song needs leadership and support, and when the assembly's song works well on its own.

Organist. The principal role of the organist is to lead the assembly's song with steady, confident playing. Secondary roles include accompanying the cantor and choir and reinforcing the mood of the celebration with instrumental music. With solid tempo, bright registration and authoritative playing, the organist leads, stimulates and inspires song rather than accompanying or following along.

Choir. Thoroughly rehearsed and more skilled than the assembly, the choir enriches and embellishes the community song. Ideally, there is more than one parish choir: adult mixed, children's, youth, and so on. The choir does not replace the assembly's singing, but enriches the assembly's song with artistic beauty and musical complexity.

Small ensemble. The ensemble does the same tasks as choir, organist and leader of song. Skill and liturgical understanding are as important to the work of the small ensemble as to the more familiar arrangement. There are great possibilities here for talented and creative leaders. Various instruments can provide color, for instance, using a string bass to ground the music like the pedal of an organ. The ensemble is a leader of prayer, with the constant challenge to turn performance into prayer.

Many well-intentioned efforts toward congregational singing have been frustrated by poor acoustics, an inadequate sound system or inappropriate instrument. A live room, a room with an echo, is best for amplifying the assembly's response. Carpeting, which absorbs sound and deadens acoustics, does not contribute to vibrant congregational song. Beautiful and easily maintained alternatives are readily available: Examples can be found in any large department store. A sound engineer should be consulted for a sound system suitable for use by cantors, lectors and homilists. An organ, whether pipe or electronic, must be designed to fit the building. Unless it is well matched to the size of the room, it is unable to stimulate congregational song.

Some assemblies have only a hymn board to guide them, some have a lector who may not have a very sure sense of music. But congregations that really sing have been taught to sing; they have been encouraged to sing with enthusiastic, good direction.

1. Can you imagine an unenthusiastic cheerleader? Or a rock concert without amplifiers? Or a birthday party at which the celebration song is whispered slowly — or worse, recited?

2. What inspires you to participate in song?

3. Does your parish employ a minister of music? If not, why not?

4. What are some ways that the organist and the leader of song encourage the assembly to sing?

5. How do you find the musically talented people in your parish and invite them into this ministry?

My life flows on in endless song

Above earth's lamentation.

I hear the real though far-off hymn

That hails a new creation.

No storm can shake my inmost calm,

While to that rock I'm clinging.

Since love is Lord of heaven and earth,

How can I keep from singing?

Through all the tumult and the strife,

I hear that music ringing;

It sounds and echoes in my soul;

How can I keep from singing?

What though the tempest 'round me roar,

I hear the truth it liveth.

What though the darkness 'round me close,

Songs in the night it giveth.

When tyrants tremble, sick with fear,

And hear their death knells ringing;

When friends rejoice both far and near,

How can I keep from singing?

Robert Lowry

The Lector

he presider or deacon usually reads the gospel and so must be, in every sense, a skillful lector. Someone other than the presider does the first readings, first, because this task requires great preparation and secondly, because the assembly benefits from hearing different voices.

The lector is the storyteller of the community. Like the elders of a tribe, the lector publicly tells the story that identifies us. We Catholics have far to go before we feel ourselves to be deeply immersed in this story, to know the scriptures intimately. In this, the lector is a leader, for before there can be a powerful telling of the story, the teller must plunge into it, learn about it, know the characters and times and places. The lector knows these not as Bible history, but as the story that gives meaning to our lives, the story that "tells us" much more than we tell it.

The assembly generally knows at once if a lector has failed to prepare a particular reading from scripture, but we seem also to be able to sense something more important: Whether the person reading is at home with the scriptures, loves them, prays with them.

Like the presider, the lector must be fully aware that this ministry is first to be part of the assembly. Like the presider, the lector needs grace in movement (in carrying the book of the scriptures in procession, and in going to and from the lectern; even in standing in silence after the reading).

The special gifts and skills of the lector have to do with drawing everyone into the scriptures. The direct preparation for this is thorough familiarity with the readings. The lector, many days before the liturgy, begins to let the reading loose, tries out its language, lets the language play back and forth both in the mind and on the lips. The lector develops a feel for the reading. The lector lets the reading into daily life: A verse runs through the mind, goes in and out with breathing. At some point it becomes important to read the scriptures that surround this particular reading, to get the context, the environment. With several readings of the scripture, spaced through the week, the lector becomes more and more free of the printed page; as a sense of how this passage is to be read (where to put emphasis, where to pause, where to be loud and where soft, where to be fast and where slow) develops, so does the ability to proclaim the reading with only an occasional glance at the printed words. Then the lector's whole manner can be directed to the listeners. Lectors should never fear "overdoing" in this regard; it is not likely to happen.

This preparation also brings out the mood of this reading, how this reading is part of our big story. A narrative from Kings has one mood, a selection from the Law in Deuteronomy another, an angry outburst from Jeremiah another. We do not read Dickens' novels, the Declaration of Independence or the sermons of Martin Luther King, Jr., in the same manner. But that does not mean that one of these is dull in comparison with another: They are interesting in different ways.

Within the liturgy, the lector also needs a sense of pace: waiting to begin until people have settled and are ready—and then making sure that they are gripped by the first words, by their sound as much as by their content. Pace within the reading is a matter of expression, interpretation. After a pause, the final "The word of the Lord" is said in a way as that invites the faith response "Thanks be to God" from the assembly.

1. Sometimes even the best lector can have a hard time because of the lighting, sound system or quality of the printed text. Check these essentials in your space.

2. What is your lector training program like? Is it ongoing?

3. What resources are available to the lectors in your parish to reinforce their reading and understanding of the scriptures?

4. What evaluation process is in place for lectors?

When you answer the call to be a minister of the word (one who proclaims the Bible readings to the assembled faith community), you enter a deeper relationship with the word of God as revealed in sacred scripture. You take upon yourself the duty and privilege of bringing the printed word to life — making it flesh, so to speak. Your ministry as reader gives voice to God's healing and strengthening word as it goes forth irrevocably to the ends of the earth, achieving the purpose for which God sent it. In a very real sense, you become a prophet — one who speaks for God. You become another John the Baptist preparing the way of the Lord, making crooked paths straight and rough places plain. You take upon yourself the task and joy of delving ever deeper into the mystery of God's presence in the world through the revealed word. You join yourself to an ancient tradition in Jewish life that sees no more worthy occupation than the study and service of God as experienced in the sacred texts. As a Christian you identify yourself with the age-old belief that God's words find their fullest expression in one perfect word: the word made flesh, Jesus the Christ.

Aelred Rosser

Servers

hen a group of any size meets to celebrate the liturgy, someone takes responsibility for freeing the presider from various details so he may give full attention to presiding. The various tasks include assisting with the book of prayers when the presider needs to read from it; helping to set the altar table with the bread and wine; helping to share the communion, both bread and cup; setting the plates and cups aside after communion and, after Mass, making sure they are clean; taking care of the candles, incense and processional cross.

Generally these tasks are taken on by two different groups of ministers: the servers (often youngsters), and the ministers of communion. Here we discuss the former and in the next article the latter.

Though we often think of servers as children who memorize their movements and words and add solemnity to the procession in and out, the need of the presider and of the whole assembly is not for mechanical help and sanctuary dressing. We need servers who know the order of the liturgy thoroughly, can anticipate each moment and need and can meet these with grace and reverence.

This is not a job description for someone who does not fully grasp the meaning of the liturgy or perceive how it flows, for someone who is limited to responding to cues. If we work with children in this ministry, it is our duty to work with them until they have a total familiarity with the ordinary order of the service and have a sense of how to move, carry things and keep stillness and silence. One advantage to having children in this role is the mere fact of engaging them in liturgy, but we should think deeply about what this says about our approach to the liturgy. The ministry of the server best meets the needs of the assembly when the servers are teen-agers or adults.

We put acolytes into service because we have a need for them. When we ask members of our community to serve as acolytes, we need to make clear what the ministry entails and offer thorough training for these responsibilities. This training ought to include not only a careful modeling of what they will be expected to do at liturgy, but of *how* they are to perform this service. Besides these mechanics, servers need to have a good sense of the liturgy as a whole, so they can be prepared for the expected and for the unexpected. The best servers are especially sensitive to the way in which they can influence the atmosphere of prayer by their presence in the sanctuary.

In most cases, only one server is needed during the liturgy itself: to hold the book for the presider and to help with the bread and wine. The processions at the beginning, before the gospel proclamation and at the end might include additional servers carrying candles and incense and cross. The seating for the acolytes should be off to one side, not beside the presider.

Since servers are concerned with books and other objects that are used in liturgy, they need an awareness of the way these things are to be handled. What these things make possible is central to our liturgy: the reading from the book, the eating of the bread and drinking from the cup, the burning of candles and of incense. In their making and their use, these things are worthy of reverence. Obviously, a parish that is concerned with the quality of these objects, using handmade candles of purest beeswax, handsomely bound books and beautiful vessels, will naturally ask the servers to do their tasks and handle these objects with reverence.

Servers, whatever their age, sing, listen and keep silence attentively, modeling the activity of the assembly. When those who have special roles regard attentiveness as important, this inspires all present to take their prayer seriously and wholeheartedly.

The question of vesture for servers often comes up, just as for lectors and ministers of communion. The answer is not based on rank, or on somehow incorporating more people into the clergy. Servers, like lectors, ministers of communion—like all ministers—are first of all members of the assembly. Rather, the question of their vesture is a matter of what is fitting, what will help the assembly's prayer. Vestments for the presider, for the deacon, sometimes for other ministers, are appropriate when they help the prayer of the assembly. Simplicity and beauty should characterize vestments as all other objects used in the liturgy. In general, the vestment that belongs to all ministers in our tradition is the alb, a white robe covering the entire body. "The more these vestments fulfill their function by their color, design and enveloping form, the less they will need the signs, slogans and symbols which an unkind history has fastened on them." (*Environment and Art in Catholic Worship*, 94)

1. Respect is the attitude an assembly expects of those who touch beautiful things or assist during solemn movements. Respect comes from the Latin: to look again, to look back. The definition indicates a learning and a remembering process. It calls forth a sense of wonder. What is it that we respect about books? Vessels? Water? Incense?

2. What is expected of the acolytes in your parish?

3. What goes into the acolyte training process? How do you get young acolytes past responding to cues and into a sense of their ministry?

4. Do you use videotaping to help acolytes see themselves in action?

Have you ever stared at the stars in the sky for so long that you stop seeing the stars and you start to daydream?

Or maybe you've sat still for a long time looking at a little baby. You watch the little one scrunch up its face and kick its feet and wave its arms and blow spit bubbles and make funny noises. And deep inside you feel love for this little baby. And maybe you wonder what it's thinking. And maybe you want to pick up the baby and hold it.

Have you ever picked up a seashell or a dried-up, empty cocoon, stared at it and said "Cool!"?

If you've ever done these things, felt this way, then you've been reverent. To be reverent means to stand in wonder before something that is beautiful and great and important and holy. To be reverent means to feel love and show respect for someone who is beautiful and great and important and holy. To be reverent we have to use our minds, our hearts and our bodies.

David Philippart

Ministers of Communion

inisters of communion help the whole community. Primarily, they make the communion rite take place in a length of time that is not out of proportion to the whole liturgy. This is not a matter of efficiency, but a recognition that its meaning cannot be separated from our experience of it in the ritual. When "going to communion" takes a long time, and so the eating and drinking together is not experienced, then the communion rite loses its association with the eucharistic prayer and the breaking of the bread. The number of ministers of communion needed, therefore, is determined by the number of communicants at a Mass.

These ministers come forward from the assembly at a moment when this movement will not be a distraction competing for attention with the breaking of the bread or the Lord's Prayer. They can come forward after the Amen of the eucharistic prayer, and be present at the table for the communion rite. Alternatively, they can come forward at the peace greeting, greeting people with the peace as they approach the table and take their places. At the table they join in singing the "Lamb of God," a litany that lasts as long as it takes to break the bread and prepare the cups.

After the presider has invited all to communion, "Blessed are those called to the banquet of the Lamb!" the ministers go as soon as possible to share the bread and cup with the rest of the assembly. It would be unwise to take a great deal of time with the communion of the ministers themselves, lest it appear like two communion services. If this seems to happen, the ministers may receive communion after everyone else. After communion, they do not return to the altar table, but take the vessels to the side. After the liturgy, they may return to clean the vessels carefully and put them away. The preparation of the bread, wine and vessels before Mass and the cleaning afterwards may be the responsibility of the sacristan, or this could be a duty of the ministers of communion.

Those selected for this ministry have, or soon acquire, the grace in movement and reverence in touch that characterizes all who minister before the assembly. Reverence in touch is especially important for ministers of communion, since their whole work involves taking in hand the vessels of bread and of wine and sharing them with everyone.

Their reverence for what they carry can be seen and felt by all: not false humility, but joy and delight in the sharing of the Lord's body and blood. This can be seen in how they pick up and carry the plate or cup, how the minister stands, as well as in how the cup or plate is later returned to a side table. It can be seen in as simple a matter as using both hands to carry the plate or cup.

Most of all, the minister of communion puts reverence into practice when giving the bread and the cup to others. By his or her eyes, smile and gentle serving of bread and cup, the minister of communion tells us this is a very special event. The minister can make us feel good to be present at this feast and remind us that our communion with the Lord is also communion with one another.

> The moment of communion is one that should be seized by both the minister and the communicant.... This is one moment when attention should be individual and total. The eyes of the minister should meet the eyes of the communicant. The minister says the words of the formula to the person (not to the air). In placing the holy bread on the palm of the communicant's hand, the minister will touch the hand. And the same will be true of the ministry of the cup. Eye contact, direct address, touching! All are a communion of person in the Lord. This means that there can be no rush. One can minister communion with reverence and dignity and personal attention and still keep the procession moving steadily. But it cannot be done in haste, or with absent-mindedness, or with frantic searchings of the approaching processional lines. (Mary Collins, *It Is Your Own Mystery: A Guide to the Communion Rite.* Washington: Liturgical Conference, 1977.)

Some parishes help this reverence, dignity and attention happen by assigning four ministers to each station: One holds the plate of bread, another is free to give attention to taking bread and giving it to the communicants; the other two ministers stand a little distance away, each with a cup of wine. Sometimes an additional minister goes from station to station refilling wine cups.

Those who take on this ministry must, above all else, know how to be truly present to others in the moment they have. They are not dispensing machines, but brothers and sisters in this very body and blood they are sharing. They not only speak their own faith in saying "The body of Christ," they call forth the faith of the communicant.

1. "Eye contact, direct address and touching" are part of the experience of sharing. At what sharing times in your life have you seen this happen? Think about homecomings, farewells, times of forgiveness, times of tragedy.

2. Do you sense any difference in receiving communion from one minister or another? Describe what a good minister of communion does that another may not.

3. What are your criteria for selecting ministers of communion?

4. Videotape the whole communion rite with the eucharistic ministers in action. View the video with someone experienced in ballet. What does that person see?

And we are changed — and are changing. We become Christ's body, bread broken for a world that is obese with materialism and still dying of malnutrition. We become a leaven in the world's bread, an agent of change that helps the reign of God to rise, fragrantly, like a loaf browning in the oven. We become Christ's blood, wine poured out in sacrifice and in celebration, poured out for the sake of a world drowning in division and still dying of thirst, a thirst for union and communion. We become the brewer's yeast, the zest that unlocks the extraordinary in the ordinary, the tingle that makes sober people giddy with joy, the sweet smell and taste of the vintage.

Such transformation, such transubstantiation — of the bread, of the wine, of you, of me, of the church, of us — such change is possible because Christ says so: "This — and you — my body. This — and you — the cup of my blood. Do this and remember me."

Do this! Made bold by this command, let us go to the table that is Christ. Let us go and fervently pray there, "Send your Spirit upon these gifts to make them holy, that they may become" — and by sharing them that we may be — "the body and blood of our Lord Jesus Christ, at whose command we celebrate this Eucharist." Then will the Spirit whisper through the church, calling each of us and all of us by those names so dear to God: The body of Christ. The blood of Christ. Then we will answer as Bishop Augustine taught us to, by saying Amen to what we are.
The body of Christ.
The body of Christ.
Amen.
Amen.
Amen.

David Philippart

Those Who Meet, Greet and Seat

he usher does something that everyone else there does too: welcoming and offering hospitality. Ushers are the community's way of being sure that this happens, being sure that the first face everyone sees at church is smiling, being sure that people sit together, being sure that strangers are welcomed and made to feel at home. Those are things everyone in the assembly has responsibility for, but the usher is one who is assigned specifically to this responsibility.

It is the usher's ministry to greet people warmly, to introduce strangers, to help people sit together, to pass out hymnals or song sheets, to care for any needs (if someone gets sick, or other emergencies), to take up the collection, to help with good order at communion and to distribute bulletins and such in the course of saying goodbye to everyone or to direct people to coffee in the parish hall.

Somehow this work can sometimes separate ushers from the rest of the assembly. In a big church with a great many people arriving all at once, ushers may feel that there is no time to be welcoming to everyone individually, and seating may be done in a way more characteristic of the theater or sports event than the Christian community. Ushers can sometimes have the impression that they have too much to do to be able to sing or pray or keep silence with the assembly.

If this seems to be so in your parish, it may be that there are too few ushers to serve the assembly's needs. In some cases, the current ushers may never have had the ministry opened up to them. In other cases, some ushers may choose to continue to perform such parts of the ministry as taking up the collection and handing out bulletins, while others are added to reinforce the ministry of hospitality.

If the decision is made to add more ushers, then, as with all ministries, the question to ask is: What kind of person is best suited to doing these things well? Two things seem to stand out.

First, the woman or man who will make a good usher has a sense of liturgical prayer. If a person is deeply aware that this kind of prayer does not involve spectators watching while a priest says Mass, then that person has one of the necessary qualifications to be an usher. Such a person will not want to see people unwelcomed or scattered here and there in the room. And that person will not want to do anything other than entering into the assembly's prayer during the liturgy itself.

Second, the person who will make a good usher has a gift for hospitality. Like the ability to read well aloud, or the ability to lead singing, this starts with something to build on. The person who will be a good usher is comfortable with welcoming the regulars and the strangers. If offering a warm greeting to a large number of people comes hard, or if the person has difficulty recalling names, then perhaps this person belongs in a different ministry. All parishes have plenty of people with exactly the gifts needed for warm, welcoming ushering—make sure to look for potential ushers among women, elderly people and teenagers.

Everything else about being an usher can be easily learned by people who have a sense of the prayer of the assembly and a sense of hospitality. Such people will be the best ones to take up a collection, to help those who don't feel well, to distribute the bulletins, to take care of any needs special to the day (a procession, a first communion).

1. We who are active in the parish may not pay much attention to the ushers because we already feel a part of the community. We may not feel the need to be welcomed. But most of the congregation isn't so easily recognized, nor so quickly made to feel at home. Maybe we should visit another parish where we are not so well known and see if we feel welcomed. We need to put ourselves into the shoes of the shy, the new-in-town, the infrequent worshiper to get a sense of what we want to look for in our ushers.

2. Join ushers in a conversation about the difference in your feeling when a hostess seats you in a restaurant you are visiting for the first time, and when a hostess recognizes you as a regular.

3. Have you ever been invited to a gathering knowing you may know only the one who invited you? Do you find it a relief when someone reaches out to welcome you? What does that mean for the ministry of the usher?

4. How do your expectations for ushers match the ushers' perception of the role? What is their view of their responsibilities in light of the *Constitution on the Sacred Liturgy?*

5. What are the criteria for choosing ushers in your parish?

6. Is a refresher course for ushers feasible as part of your parish Ministries Day?

Yours is the first

of Christ's face to greet God's people

as they assemble for prayer.

Your greeting of welcome

is the first wish that "The Lord be with you!"

Yours is the word

that welcomes the stranger to be at home,

or the silence

that makes of our assembly a foreign land.

Yours is the task of discretion:

Knowing how to welcome,

and when and where to seat the latecomer.

Yours may be the last word

that ushers the community

to its week of work

in the Lord's vineyard.

Yours is the Lord's face and voice

for those who enter and depart

the holy ground of prayer.

Austin Fleming

Writers

hose who minister by writing are the ones who craft any introductory comments and sometimes the announcements. Writers also have responsibility for creating or choosing texts for several other elements in the liturgy. These include:

The penitential rite. Three forms of this rite are offered in the sacramentary. These are intended to suggest ways in which this rite can be done and to offer examples of the words that can be used. Depending on the season of the year, planners give more or less emphasis to the penitential rite. Texts may be selected from those offered, or new texts composed. It is important that those doing this work know that the penitential rite is not an examination of conscience, nor an act of contrition, but praise of God's unfailing mercy and love for us. It may be shaped by the mood of the season, but is not a "mini-homily." It most often takes the form of a litany and needs to do its work in few words.

Introductions to the readings. These should be used only if needed to set the stage: to place the reading in some context, to identify a place or character. Even so, they should not be merely information, but invitations to become involved in the reading. Introductions are hardly ever necessary, should never summarize the reading, and work best when they pose questions that stir the assembly's interest in the forthcoming reading.

The prayers of intercession (or petitions, or prayers of the faithful). This prayer is a litany. Litanies "work" because of the strong repetition of the refrain and the rhythm of the leader's lines between the refrains. Ordinarily, litanies are sung. The refrain, the people's part, will be stronger if it is not changed from week to week; possibly it can be varied with the seasons. The refrain will be stronger if the words that lead into it have a pattern that tells the assembly to be ready. Writers can build a collection of beautiful intercessory prayers from various traditions, especially from the Byzantine liturgy, and draw freely on these. The language is important: the flow of the words, the beauty of the expression—not to mention correct grammar! The content is important: neither so general that the thrust of the gospel in our lives is obscured nor so particular that we lose

sight of the universal needs. Often it works well to select a few petitions from those that have served through many centuries, and to write one or two others that speak of immediate needs and reflect the mood of the present. The language of scripture, and in particular of the scriptures of the current season, can be a source of words and phrases that help to shape these prayers. The prayers of intercession ought always to give a sense of the support the churches give to one another throughout the world in our constant prayer, and a sense of the special responsibility we have to pray for those in power and for those who are poor and in any need, and finally to pray for this assembly as a community with its own special needs.

Invitations. The writers can help the presider and the deacon by suggesting forms for the invitations: the deacon's invitation to the assembly to join in the memorial acclamation and in the peace greeting, the presider's invitation to all to come to the holy communion and the deacon's words of dismissal at the end of the liturgy. As invitations, these should not ordinarily be read, so the writer's task is to suggest very brief forms that allow ministers to make these invitations very personal and direct.

Other texts. The writers will find it useful to become thoroughly familiar with the sacramentary so that they can suggest choices in texts for the preface and for the final blessing. Furthermore, there are thirteen texts for the eucharistic prayer in the Roman rite. Anyone involved in determining choices should be deeply familiar with this central prayer and the reasons for using different prayers on different occasions.

Good writers are rare. Care for words—their power, their beauty—and patience in composing are essential. So is a sensitivity that guides the writer to use inclusive language at all times. This need not sound awkward. Awkwardness comes when a reader adds "and she" to every "he," "or her" to every "his," on the spot. Many texts that sound exclusive need to be recast completely rather than simply adjusted. Texts composed locally can be inclusive without being self-conscious.

1. In your parish, what is the process for choosing or composing texts? How many people are involved?

2. Do presider and planners work together to choose the texts of the liturgies and inform other ministers of their choices?

3. What efforts are made to recruit poets and people with the ability to craft appealing and effective sentences?

I write the way I do because (not though) I am a Catholic. This is a fact and nothing covers it like the bald statement. However, I am a Catholic peculiarly possessed of the modern consciousness, that thing Jung describes as unhistorical, solitary, and guilty. To possess this *within* the Church is to bear a burden, the necessary burden for the conscious Catholic. It's to feel the contemporary situation at the ultimate level. I think that the Church is the only thing that is going to make the terrible world we are coming to endurable; the only thing that makes the Church endurable is that it is somehow the body of Christ and that on this we are fed. It seems to be a fact that you have to suffer as much from the Church as for it but if you believe in the divinity of Christ, you have to cherish the world at the same time that you struggle to endure it.

Flannery O'Connor

No one should seek an end to necessary and fundamental rubrical or ceremonial directions — as no one should be so arrogant as to create their own liturgy. But we should welcome the freedom and flexibility built into the liturgical reform, so that the celebration in the Christian community may become a living and real thing, the sign of genuine prayer and faith.

Frederick R. McManus

Sacristans and Artists

These ministers' work and presence are apparent in the room and in the things that are seen and touched within the liturgy. Those who clean and polish, as much as those who create vestments and hangings, come from the assembly to care for a specific need: to fashion a place that helps people pray together. The two groups need to stay close in their thinking and in their work. Both need a clear vision of the overall goal: an environment that is hospitable, welcoming, clean, human; an environment that is beautiful, that in itself points beyond to the awe and wonder that foster our prayer; an environment that is honest, the work of caring people.

These ministers should have a sense of the objects we use in our prayer as common objects. We are not a church that uses "cult objects" in order to pray. Our prayer does not depend on anyone manufacturing anything that is not also needed in the course of simple human life. We sit on benches and chairs; we place a good loaf of bread on a plate; we put wine in a cup; plate and cup rest on a table covered with good fabric; we listen to scriptures read from a handsome book; we immerse new members of the community in ordinary water; we help to center our attention and prayer with burning candles and with vestments and hangings. But all of these—benches, bread, wine, table and cloth, book, water, candle, fabric—are things of everyday life. We sit, we eat bread and drink wine, we read, we bathe and dress in the course of daily life. We do not succeed in prayer by seeming to separate the bread of the Mass from the bread of our dinner table: Rather, we succeed by making all these things with strength, simplicity and great beauty. This does not bring down the Mass, but proclaims that ours is a faith forever bound up with the stuff of everyday life, with incarnation.

Those who select the benches and vessels and vestments and all else look to artisans who fashion wood and clay and glass and fabric with care and dignity. Seldom, if ever, do they choose to look to those who mass-produce church goods. The local church's artists may be able to supply some of the objects to be used in the worship space and in the liturgy, but generally the parish does best to seek out and commission competent craftspeople and artists to create in textiles, clay, wood, glass and metal.

Like the musicians, who must not only be schooled in music but must have a vital sense of liturgy, the artists must know not only what is beautiful but what is capable of serving their particular community's prayer. A direct application of this is in the care that these ministers have for the seasons of the liturgical year. They seek ways in which Lent, for example, can be seen to be present in the room. What are its colors, textures, shapes, objects? Answers depend on exploring the scriptures and hymns and devotions of the season, on a sense of what people's lives are like during the weeks of this season, on respect for the ways that this particular parish has housed Lent in the past and for an appreciation of those among us who are about to be initiated into our church. Further, answers depend on sensitivity to the impressions made over the weeks of the seasons, and on making evaluations and decisions about what becomes a regular part of the season so that over the years we become more and more at home in our Lent.

Both sacristans and artists need a sense of the whole room, not the sanctuary alone, as important for worship.

> Suitable decoration need not and should not be confined to the altar area, since the unity of the celebration space and the active participation of the entire assembly are fundamental principles. The negative aspect of this attention invites a thorough housecleaning in which superfluities, things that have no use or are no longer in use, are removed. Both beauty and simplicity demand careful attention to each piece of furniture, each object, each decorative element, as well as the whole ensemble, so that there is no clutter, no crowding. These various objects and elements must be able to breathe and function without being smothered to excess.
> (*Environment and Art in Catholic Worship,* 103)

The work of the sacristans of a parish ideally is more than weekly and monthly cleaning. A sacristan is needed before and between the weekend Masses in a parish. Care for the condition of the whole room where liturgy is celebrated, as well as for the vestments, vessels, candles, bread and wine for each celebration of the eucharist, is best done by one person or by sharing among several persons. This relieves the presider and other ministers of such tasks in the crucial moments before and after the liturgy and heightens awareness of our shared tasks in the liturgy.

1. The sacristans are the homemakers of the parish, of the house of the church. List three or four qualities that are desirable in a homemaker.

2. Very frequently there are gifted artists and crafts-people in our parishes or in the larger community, but because we've been satisfied with mass-produced church goods, many of the finest artists and crafts-people have been led to believe that their gifts are not needed. How can you better use these talented people in your parish?

3. What do you do about altar bread each week?

4. How much are the sacristans a part of your whole liturgy picture? What kind of qualifications should a sacristan have?

5. What commissions has your parish given recently to artists or craftspeople? How were they chosen?

Sacristans must be zealous in their commitment to fostering the growth of the local church. This happens through the setting up of liturgical elements, but also through the sharing of responsibilities with children and adults, the friendly supervision of all aspects of the work. With the gifts of all members so central to the vitality of the church, the days when a sacristan could claim the sacristy as a personal fiefdom are long gone.

Sacristans may be of any age and either gender. All that counts is the ability to perform and enjoy the tasks. The role of sacristan was once reserved to the ordained. By this century, it had been taken over mostly by women — boys were servers and girls were junior sacristans. Now all are welcome — young and old, male and female — and the diversity of our individual gifts brings fresh approaches to this work. Parishes that engage large numbers of volunteers in such projects as decorating for Christmas and Easter will want to include whole households.

G. Thomas Ryan

The Church has need of saints, yes, but also of artists, of skilled and good artists. Both saints and artists are a witness of the living Spirit of Christ. Yours is the trust and the privilege of giving to the Church new artists who will express and advance the holiness of the Church.

Pope Paul VI

Other Ministers

In a ritual such as the parish Sunday eucharist or the celebration of a wedding, many gifts are shared. Most of these ministries we have discussed. Some others, no less important, are mentioned briefly here.

Bread bakers. "The nature of the sign demands that the material for the eucharistic celebration appear as actual food. The eucharistic bread, even though unleavened, should therefore be made in such a way that the priest can break it and distribute the parts to at least some of the faithful." (*General Instruction of the Roman Missal,* 283) To carry out this norm—because it makes such good common sense—a parish will see that "the work of human hands" is something local, a ministry intimately bound up with the eucharist.

Movement and gesture. There is need for those with sensitivity to movement to help all the ministries. The assembly, the presider, the lector, the acolytes and so on: All of these move in doing their parts in the prayer, all of them have occasions to use gesture. Yet few are aware of the power and beauty of movement and gesture when done well, or the power they have to distract when done poorly. Ministers can learn to make their movements and their gestures a full part of the liturgy. This is not a matter of learning to walk or genuflect the way somebody else walks or genuflects: Rather, an artist can lead each person to his or her own strongest expression in these gestures.

Planners and coordinators. This ministry is commonly exercised by the liturgy committee or team. More and more, the planning means work with the seasons of the liturgical year and with the Sundays of Ordinary Time. It also means planning for the parish's various sacramental celebrations, such as communal penance services, confirmation, weddings. Some of these sacramental celebrations may be seen as fitting more and more into the seasons, for example, communal anointing of the sick during Eastertime; other celebrations may become the responsibility of special groups whose ministry is to work with the persons involved in a wedding, a funeral, a baptism. Apart from planning, there is the ongoing work of coordinating, which means establishing some structures to see to the recruiting, training and scheduling of all the ministers. Ideally, each ministry cares for its own recruiting and training, as well as for opportunities for reflection, prayer and socializing together.

Coordination. In large parishes it is often helpful to have someone present before the Sunday Masses simply to make sure that the assigned ministers are present, that they come together for a few moments of prayer, that each knows about any special planning that will touch on that Sunday's liturgy. This is an especially important ministry when there are baptisms, first communions, the use of audio-visual materials, a dramatic presentation of one of the scriptures, and so on.

Today many parishes have hired or are considering hiring a parish liturgy director. This person's job is not to replace any of the ministries, but to care for all of them and to contribute the time, creativity and imagination that will enable all the parish to pray the liturgy and make it their own through the years.

1. After instituting a variety of ministries in the parish and making creative plans for worship, there is still the task of bringing it all together. Sometimes the best of plans can fail because there is no one to orchestrate the effort. Who instructs the ministers about the liturgy of the season or the feast? Who takes responsibility for the coordination?

2. Does your parish make its own eucharistic bread? It takes the leadership of a coordinator (or scheduler) and the work of a number of people who will do the mixing and kneading and baking. Might you volunteer to be a baker in your parish? Or, if the parish doesn't yet bake its own bread, might you be the coordinator who gets things started?

Ministers must not clericalize the liturgy. The liturgy belongs to no one but the church, Christ's body, which is both subject and agent of every liturgical act. Since every liturgical act is an ecclesial act, liturgical ministers of whatever order are servants of this act inasmuch as they are servants of the ecclesial assembly. They must, moreover, not only be so but appear to be so.

Thomas Simons and James Fitzpatrick

❖

The liturgy is not a theater where actors on stage take bows and applause at curtain call. It is an arena of holy ground where God's people stand naked and empty-handed in the Creator's presence. Our time and prayer in this holy place are served by sinners like ourselves whose only vesture is ours, too: We are all clothed in Christ as the new creation. These servants point the way for all who assemble. Their proximity to table and ambo is one of service, not priority. The servants are seen and heard so that all might see and hear the Lord among us. If they are the first to be served from the table, it is so they might be nourished for the serving of others. They are distinguished not so much by what they do, but by whose work they become in its doing.

Austin Fleming

❖

It is every artisan's hope that what is produced will be considered beautiful both in its function and in its being. For the potter who creates the most utilitarian objects — cups, vases, bowls, teapots — there is a constant challenge (and opportunity) to put beauty into work. This is our modest way of reaffirming the beauty of the large creation. "Beauty will save the world," says Father Zosima in *The Brothers Karamazov,* and in that rather large task of world salvation the artist plays a modest but real role: to create epiphanies of beauty on the mundane surrounding of everyday life.

Cecilia Davis Cunningham

The Mass

The Mass is the most familiar of our rituals. In this section we approach the Mass simply as a ritual.

Liturgy planners and ministers of the assembly, as much as if not more than other Catholics, need to be mindful of other dimensions. The theology and spirituality of the Mass give us images of its place in the life of the church and in the life of the participating individuals. Some of these dimensions are more accessible when we look at the unfolding of the Mass as a ritual from beginning to end: its opening rites, the proclamation of the word, the liturgy of the eucharist and the concluding rites. We need to have a grasp of how the Mass is a ritual and of how the good use of that ritual is vital to us.

Eucharist on Sunday

uch of what has been said of ritual, of the elements of common prayer and of ministries comes together in considering the Sunday eucharist. The next pages look at the elements of this one liturgy. Later we will look at the liturgies of the sacraments and other occasions.

The Mass brings together two rituals that once existed separately: a liturgy of the word, and a liturgy of the eucharist. Each is influenced by its association with the other. In addition, various rites help us with transitions: as we move from our various homes and individual lives into this time of prayer together (preparation rites); as we move from word to eucharist (preparation of the gifts); and finally as we move from the prayer toward home (concluding rites).

All of this is quite natural. People seek familiar ways to gather and go about their prayer. From their very early times, Christians have gathered to break bread on the first day of the week, Sunday, or the Lord's day as they came to call it. The day after the Jewish Sabbath day, which is the seventh and last day of the week, was associated with the eighth day, the day beyond time, the day of salvation. Marking this day kept the familiar rhythm of the seven-day week. Christians assembled to give thanks and praise and share the holy communion. When Christians gathered on other days of the week in their households or with larger groups, it would be to read scripture, to pray and to sing hymns, but not for eucharist.

In the course of the centuries, many things altered this practice. Very early, the rites of word and of eucharist were joined. In stages, the celebration of word and eucharist together, our Mass, spread to the weekdays. Also in stages, the Mass as the action of the assembly gave way to the Mass as the ceremony of the presider, and it made little difference whether people were present or how they participated. The Protestant reformers for the most part did away with the practice of Mass on weekdays. Some of their followers went even further and had eucharist on Sunday only a few times a year.

Through all this and much more, most churches retained the association of the eucharist with Sunday. Sometimes this association has been weak, and sometimes it has been maintained only through the sense of the "Sunday obligation," but it is part of our tradition that won't go away. If anything, recent practice and teaching have led toward enriching the weekdays at home and in the parish with Morning and Evening Prayer, strengthening the tie between Sunday and the community's celebration of eucharist.

The first day of the week, Sunday, and the gathering for the breaking of the bread belong together. Each enhances the other. The day, kept in some way as sign of the new creation and of the freedom from death and sin, calls for eucharist. Eucharist, as proclamation of the death and resurrection of the Lord until he comes, needs Sunday, the day of the Lord kept holy by the people. That means something more than trying to work Mass into a busy schedule. It means that Sunday makes way: It sets us free from our million cares, free to pray over them, free to listen to the scriptures, free to remember and celebrate what sometimes gets lost in the week. We are human. We are active but need contemplation too. We need the rhythm of the one day set off against the other six.

Sunday—a day of liberation, a day of space, a time of memory, a time for recreation, a space to gather, a place for gathering, a gathering for worship in thankfulness.

In the end, everything has to work together: individual and family efforts to make Sunday special and to lead up to and away from the Mass, and the efforts of liturgy planners and ministers to do liturgy so well that all present know that they do the eucharist together.

1. Do you anticipate Sunday? Do you gather yourself, your family, your community on this day? What does Sunday feel like? What would you like it to feel like?

2. Eucharist on Sunday demands not only a serious, thorough planning of the liturgy, but a continuing effort to renew the importance of Sunday as the Lord's day. Good Sunday worship demands that Christians make the Lord's day something different in their lives. What are some practical ways to make Sunday into the Lord's Day for your family and for your parish?

3. We may criticize people who look at Sunday Mass simply as an obligation, but do we support that attitude in the way we care for the liturgy?

4. How is Sunday Mass celebrated differently than weekday Mass?

The appreciation of Sunday has been all of a piece with Christians' perception of time itself. To the degree that Christians' concept of the "supernatural" located the life of God in another time and another place, Sunday became a radically different day. To the degree that Christians have adopted the cultural image of time and history, Sunday become a merely cultural institution: time off, or time for overtime. To the degree, however, that we understand the Gospel to offer us an alternative vision of the future — and thus to demand an alternative set of present values, an alternative way of living in time — Sunday itself will have a specifically Christian meaning, embodying that vision, proleptic of that future, and gathering to itself those whose loyalties are to that alternative way of living in time.

Mark Searle

In the course of the Christian centuries, Sunday has remained a stable point of reference, lending a fixed rhythm to Christian lives lived in widely different circumstances of time and place. Yet, for all its stability, it has come to mean many different things. This was true even in the early centuries, as the different names given to Sunday attest; "the first day of the week," "the Lord's day," "the eighth day," to mention the most common. Later, in the Middle Ages, it came also to be spoken of analogously as the Sabbath. Each of these names, plus the kind of observances considered appropriate for this day, reflect different insights into the mystery of Sunday.

Mark Searle

Gathering

e are not like television sets, able to change from one channel to another in seconds. We need to pass more slowly from one time to the next. Sometimes the way we construct spaces helps this: We have lobbies, entrance ways, yards, waiting rooms and other assorted in-between spaces. We do the same with our time: small talk that often needs to come before the business at hand, the whole system we have for leading up to saying goodbye. We help each other in and out of moments together.

People who meet to pray are no different. The rites that come before we begin the scripture readings at Mass are introductions of one sort or another, preliminaries, ways to ease into this activity. But even before we come to the entrance hymn, or the sign of the cross together, we have the less formal rituals of gathering: all that happens and all that surrounds us from the time we walk toward the church until the first hymn.

These informal moments are crucial. It is here that the ushers are important as greeters, hosts, ministers of hospitality. It is here that all must be in readiness for the liturgy, without last-minute dashing around by any of the ministers. The whole atmosphere must be one of welcoming, open to those who would like to sit or kneel quietly and to those who exchange greetings with friends. Sometimes there is music for all to practice, sometimes instrumentalists might provide music as people gather. Lighting is also important (here and throughout the liturgy) in the atmosphere that it sets and in the emphasis that it lends. The decor should evoke within us a sense of the season or day. The informal moments end when the word of welcome is spoken by song leader, cantor, usher or commentator. Then we may be asked to stand and sing together. This is not a song "to welcome our celebrant." The singing is to "deepen the unity of the people, and introduce them to the mystery of the season or feast" (*General Instruction of the Roman Missal*, 25).

"The parts preceding the liturgy of the word, namely, the entrances, greeting, penitential rite, Kyrie, Gloria, and opening prayer or collect, have the character of introduction and preparation. The purpose of these rites is to help the assembled people make themselves a worshiping community and to prepare them for listening to God's word and celebrating the eucharist." (*General Instruction*, 24)

This note on the character of these rites is extremely important. The rites must be seen as that which they intend: introduction, preparation, helping people make themselves a worshiping community. If this is so, then the parts of the entrance rite are not just so many units to run through one after the other. They must work so that their purpose is achieved: At the end of the entrance rites, when we sit to hear the scriptures, we feel like a community and we have picked up something of the mood for today's liturgy of the word. Note that it is something of the mood that we receive, not a summary of what is to come through the stating of themes.

The *Directory for Masses with Children* recognizes that our introductory rites are too crowded with small pieces that do not do their work well. "It is sometimes proper to omit one or the other element of the introductory rites or perhaps to enlarge one of the elements. There should always be at least some introductory element, which is completed by the opening prayer or collect." (40) The direction pointed out here will be more widely applied in the future, as the introductory notes of the forthcoming sacramentary indicate. Balance, flow and timing are qualities to look for. The whole introductory rite is to be just that: an introduction. Introductions, though, can easily grow to be events in themselves.

Singing together, good processional instrumental music, a beautiful procession through the assembly, a strong greeting and the sign of the cross as a common gesture—these and the silence leading to the prayer have the potential to build a sense of being together at prayer. Even so, they can take on different characters and emphases with the seasons. Pace is extremely important.

Each of the elements of the introductory rites needs to be well understood by planners. For example, the penitential rite contains a litany of praise for God's loving kindness to us, not a confession of certain sins. The Gloria demands to be sung; the long text is difficult to recite well and with energy.

1. How would you describe the mood in the church right before Mass begins? Commotion? Anxious anticipation? Peacefulness? Coldness?

2. How is the time before Mass used in your parish? Remember: Those few minutes before Mass begins are precious moments to prepare ministers and assembly for worship. For the ministers, the time before Mass should include a final check of responsibilities, but beyond that, there should be a quiet time, perhaps a moment of prayer together. The assembly may need a music rehearsal or a short introduction to the liturgy of the day. If so, there should usually be some silence or a reflective prelude before the procession begins.

3. Latecomers to Mass: Is this just a little problem that will never go away, or is it a real obstacle to good liturgy that must be solved?

At this table we put aside every worldly separation based on culture, class, or other differences. Baptized, we no longer admit to distinctions based on age or sex or race or wealth. This communion is why all prejudice, all racism, all sexism, all deference to wealth and power must be banished from our parishes, our homes, and our lives. This communion is why we will not call enemies those who are human is like ourselves. This communion is why we will not commit the world's resources to an escalating arms race while the poor die. We cannot. Not when we have feasted here on the "body broken" and "blood poured out" for the life of the world.

Cardinal Joseph Bernardin

❖

What do people do when they assemble to worship? They seek out each other's company to acknowledge the Love the surrounds them, attracts them, impels them. If they live their lives regularly in the presence of the Holy and gather on Sunday to do the same in common, coming together in this way makes eminently good sense. If they do not live their lives in God's presence, regular assembly may lead to a posture of awe, but this is by no means assured.

Gerard S. Sloyan

The Liturgy of the Word: I

he way Christians tell their story in ritual owes much to the ritual storytelling of the Jewish communities at the time of Jesus. The central aspect of this was, and is, the reading of the scriptures. These writings contain the narratives, poetry, prophecy, laws and letters that make up our story. The liturgy of the word simply provides a structure to allow the reading and the listening to be done effectively, beautifully and in common.

The pattern that has come down to us calls for two or three readings from the scriptures, with the last one taken from the gospels. The elements surrounding the scripture readings assists the assembly in their listening, reflecting and responding to the God who speaks through the readings. There is an overall flow to this rite: scripture, silence, psalm, scripture, silence. Then the gospel, surrounded with acclamation, and the homily. The rite concludes with the prayers of intercession. Without care, though, the entire rite can become one little group of words added to another. The flowing back-and-forth of word, silence and music gives this rite its rhythm. Each element must be presented and must be done well. And, just as in music, everything depends on their relationship: on the pace that puts everything together and gives a sense of the whole.

Our church attaches great importance to the basic ritual of reading and listening. Whether we gather for eucharist, for baptism or for another rite, the church's book is opened and read. In the current arrangement of the scripture readings (that is what the lectionary is), the Sundays of Ordinary Time are when we read continuously through the New Testament letters in the second reading and through the gospels: Matthew in Year A, Mark in Year B, Luke in Year C. During the special seasons of the year, this continuous reading is broken as we turn to those passages that are the very foundation of Advent and Christmastime, Lent and Eastertime.

It is the task of lectors, deacons and priests to read the scriptures so that they command the attention of all. It is the task of the assembly to listen. Reading along with the lector is not listening. We gain far more if we fix our gaze on the reader and cling to every word, repeating some of the words within our hearts.

Through the year-in, year-out listening to our scriptures, we are formed, challenged, comforted and embraced by God's word. The homilist—facing the Sunday's readings in the context of the readings of the whole season or the continuous reading of Ordinary Time—is to make certain that the word and community confront each other.

The churches have attached great importance to the continuous telling of the story, year-in and year-out, through the centuries. The proclaimed scriptures help us to remember who we are. The proclamation in the midst of the assembly makes quite a different point than the same reading done by every individual, alone in their homes. The scriptures for the coming Sunday should be readily available for reading, reflection and discussion by individuals and families as preparation for coming to the liturgy. The assembly comes alive to the fuller dimensions of the readings when they have attuned themselves by their own preparation of the texts at home. Planners and homilists need a sense of the way the scriptures are used through the three cycles of the lectionary. They need to be aware, for example, of Year A as the "Year of Matthew," of the way the scriptures of each season (Advent, Christmastime, Lent, Eastertime) have their own integrity, of the flow of the continuous reading of Paul's letters and of the gospels through the Sundays of Ordinary Time.

It is not generally effective to isolate one Sunday from another by seeking some "theme" in each one. Instead, planners consider the overall spirit or mood of the various liturgical seasons and read each Sunday's scriptures in that spirit. During Ordinary Time, planners need to have a feeling for just that: the ordinary, the way the story continues from week to week.

It is not, then, a matter of deciding that the scriptures today are about justice, therefore let us find songs about justice, a homily about justice, banners about justice and so on. It is rather to have a feeling that these scriptures, which are about many things on many levels, justice being one of them, are—if well told—but one expression and experience of an Advent or of the course of the story in August. The telling of the story in this rite is never intended to take out all the poetry, to say that the scripture means just this or just that. We stick with the scriptures and not books of theology or lives of saints precisely because they open up, rather than limit and define. They are not historical data or somebody else's piety. They are free to be about you, about me, about anyone, about us. They can be my story, our story, when as the church we hear and reflect.

1. The way we celebrate the liturgy of the word reveals our understanding of the books we use in ritual. If our understanding of the books is weak, we keep a habit of moving nonstop from one text to the next, as if that's all it would take for good worship, never leaving room for silence, reflection, or the pacing of the elements together. Neither the lectionary nor the sacramentary are automatic ritual formulas. They are there to be listened to, responded to, not mechanically read through. How have you experienced this to be true?

2. What do missalettes do to the rhythm and flow of the liturgy of the word? How do missalettes lock people into an individualistic piety within the liturgy?

In Luke 7, after John the Baptist raises his christological question through his disciples whether Jesus is the Christ, and after Jesus answers with specificity that "the blind see, the lame walk, lepers are cleansed, the dead are raised, and the poor rejoice," Jesus adds, "blessed is the one who is not scandalized by me" (v. 23). Or as I have rendered it, "lucky are you, if you are not upset." The theological scandal of biblical faith, especially when rendered into political, economic issues, is indeed upsetting.

How is a pastor to give voice to this scandal in a society that is hostile to it, in a church that is often unwilling to host the scandal, and when we ourselves as teachers and pastors of the church are somewhat queasy about the scandal as it touches our own lives? How can the radical dimension of the Bible as it touches public reality be heard in the church?

Walter J. Burghardt, SJ

The Liturgy of the Word: 2

n this section and the next we will look at each of the movements of the ordinary structure of the liturgy of the word.

The first reading. Ordinarily, the Sunday liturgy has two scripture readings before the gospel. The first of these is usually from the Hebrew Scriptures and ordinarily has some relationship to the day's gospel. This relationship is not one of opposition, of the "old" and the "new," of the "partial" and the "complete," the "shadow" and the "reality." Rather, it is a relationship of the continuity "of our faith with the earlier covenant." (This is the emphasis in the 1975 Vatican guidelines for Jewish-Catholic relations.) The use of the Hebrew Scriptures in our Sunday liturgies says clearly that our faith did not originate in Jesus, that in fact we will only understand Jesus and his preaching and deeds when we are immersed in the whole of the scriptures which we call holy, especially those which formed Jesus himself. Introductory comments to this scripture sometimes give the impression that its only role is to set us up for the real thing. That is not true. In care of preparation, in attention from the assembly, the first reading is as important as those that follow. How it is handled may determine whether the readings that follow are listened to.

Silence. The *General Instruction of the Roman Missal* notes that there are many times when silence is to be part of the ritual. Among these is a silence after each of the first two readings and a silence after the homily. It is needed when the scripture has been proclaimed and listened to well: There is something to reflect on, an appreciation for a quiet moment to turn it over or to let one word or phrase echo in one's mind. It is silence together—for all the ministers and everyone in the assembly. No one is busy getting music or books or papers ready or seating latecomers. When the length of the silence is the same week after week, there is no nervous wondering when it will end. It becomes a habit.

Responsorial psalm. The responsorial psalm grows out of the silence. It does not come as a sharp break. It is not a time to have a book in hand. The psalm simply flows from the silence without announcement or disturbance. The style of the music both continues the reflection and draws in the active participation of the assembly. Groups that are getting accustomed to full participation in the liturgy sometimes do well to use the same refrain on each Sunday of a liturgical season, and not many for Ordinary Time: In word and in melody these refrains pick up the mood of the time and tie the weeks together. This also frees the assembly from the necessity of printed music, thus encouraging better reflection and response. Seasonal psalms and refrains are found in the lectionary. Groups with an established participatory style can deepen their appreciation of the psalm as integral to the scripture of the day. Many sturdy, singable settings are available for the psalm refrains. Often the proper psalm refrain becomes a mantra carrying the Sunday scriptures through the week in the hearts of the faithful. The rhythm of the liturgy of the word makes it obvious that singing is necessary here, not another set of spoken words.

Second reading. The second readings come from the letters of Paul and others. During the seasons these are specially selected. During Ordinary Time, we have a continuous reading from the letters, week by week, that makes no effort to relate this text to the first reading or to the gospel: It is simply a progression through the epistles. This can call for extra efforts of preparation by the lector, especially when it is helpful to make a connection between this reading and the selection read the week before. The fact that this second reading follows its own path through one portion of scripture also suggests that a different lector read it, making it all the more obvious that there is not a unifying theme among the elements of the story that are read, but that we find ourselves at different places in the gradual movement through the whole of the scriptures. We do not need a common theme to unite the three readings. We are capable of keeping separate strands going at the same time. We do this easily enough with comic strips, soap operas and developing stories from the front pages.

Silence. A period of silence and stillness follows the reading. It is needed not only for reflection, but to allow the acclamation and gospel to be strong. The contrast is very important.

1. How often is the first reading used as the primary source for the preaching where you are?

2. How often does the homilist preach on the psalm of the day or work in references to the psalm in the preaching?

In a sense, our liturgy is a higher form of silence. It is pervaded by an awed sense of the grandeur of God which resists description and surpasses all expression. The individual is silent. We do not bring forth our own words. Our saying the consecrated words is in essence an act of listening to what they convey. The Spirit of Israel speaks, the self is silent.

Twofold is the meaning of silence. One, the abstinence from speech, the absence of sound. Two, inner silence, the absence of self concern, stillness. One may articulate words with the voice and yet be inwardly silent. One may abstain from uttering any sound and yet be overbearing.

Both are inadequate: our speech as well as our silence. Yet there is a level that goes beyond both: the level of song. "There are three ways in which one expresses deep sorrow: the person on the lowest level cries; the person on the second level is silent; the person on the highest level knows how to turn sorrow into song." True prayer is a song.

Abraham Joshua Heschel

Liturgy of the Word: 3

cclamation. "The acclamations are shouts of joy which arise from the whole assembly as forceful and meaningful assents to God's word and action. They are important because they make some of the most significant moments of the Mass (gospel, eucharistic prayer, Lord's Prayer) stand out. It is of their nature that they should be rhythmically strong, melodically appealing, and affirmative. The people should know the acclamations by heart in order to sing them spontaneously." (*Music in Catholic Worship,* 53) The *General Instruction* reinforces this by noting that when the alleluia is not sung, it may be omitted: You can't make an acclamation without raising the voice in some way, either shouting or singing. The alleluia, or some other acclamation during Lent, breaks the silence with sound and with movement. The acclamation is really not only the singing, it is also the solemn procession with the book of the gospels, accompanied by candles or by incense, to the ambo, as well as the movement of the assembly from sitting to standing to indicate both honor to the gospel and a more formal stance of attention. The acclamation is a needed moment after the listening and reflection. With just a brief introduction from the organ or sung introduction from the cantor, everyone takes up the alleluia.

Gospel. The reading of the gospel begins with the greeting from the presider or deacon, the solemn announcement and response with the sign of the cross on forehead, lips and heart. At its conclusion, there is a special response, and the one who has read may kiss the book. Candles and incense to honor the gospel add to this moment. All these elements make it crucial that the reader give every effort to these familiar stories so their power can be felt.

Homily. The presider or deacon has the task of sharing reflections on the day's scriptures. This is not a time-out but is as much a part of our liturgy together as anything else. The ways in which the story is truly ours are opened up here. The homily is a kind of dialogue with the story, with the scriptures of the day. Attention is demanded of the assembly and hard work in preparation and delivery from the homilist.

Silence. When the homilist is seated, there is a time of silence and stillness for reflection.

Creed. On Sundays and great feasts, the creed is recited after the homily. Sometimes this is presented as an opportunity to respond to the readings and homily with an affirmation of faith. However, it is in fact very difficult to make such a long formula feel like an affirmation. It often comes across as an interruption when the other parts of the liturgy of the word have been done well.

General intercessions. The prayer that concludes the liturgy of the word is an ancient way of praying, a litany, whose context is equally ancient and very human: intercession, placing our condition before our God. This prayer comes at what seems to be the right moment: The listening and reflecting are finished, the church has been gathered together by God's word, and people have been quiet, except for brief acclamations, for some time now. A very involving prayer is needed, and that is what the general intercessions intend. There is the briefest invitation from the presider, then the litany of petitions begins. Litanies work best when they are sung rather than recited because they depend so much on the strength of the repetition. More than the same words coming over and over again, we need the same sounds and the flow that music can give, as when the litany of the saints or of the Blessed Virgin is chanted with the strong "Ora pro nobis" — "Pray for us" — coming again and again and again. The repeated refrain of the assembly is the prayer, with the intercession providing motive. In the intercessions, the assembly is asked to pray for the church, for authorities, for the oppressed, for the local community. The litany of the intercessions needs to be strong in its rhythm, giving support to the feeling of a community at prayer, a community directed to the service of the world. It is the prayer of the church and should feel and sound like it. At the end, the presider draws the prayer to a brief conclusion.

1. The gospel acclamation can be enhanced when the motion of standing up is completed with a gesture of praise, as when all lift their arms together at a given moment in the singing.

2. How does a congregation build a set of acclamations that are truly engaging?

3. How can a congregation come to appreciate silence?

4. How attractive is the parish's book of scriptures?

5. What process is in place for evaluating homilies?

6. How can the general intercessions best be prepared and prayed?

7. Think about the quality of the language used in the invocations. Are images used? Are evocative words used? Is a consistent format used throughout the set of intercessions? Does each invocation end with an actual invitation "Let us" so that the assembly knows clearly when to give the prayer "Lord..."?

What is this place where we are meeting?

Only a house, the earth its floor.

Walls and a roof, sheltering people,

windows for light, an open door.

Yet it becomes a body that lives

when we are gathered here,

and know our God is near.

Words from afar, stars that are falling,

Sparks that are sown in us like seed:

names for our God, dreams, signs and wonders

sent from the past are all we need.

We in this place remember and speak

Again what we have heard:

God's free redeeming word.

And we accept bread at his table,

broken and shared, a living sign.

Here in this world, dying and living,

we are each other's bread and wine.

This is the place where we can receive

What we need to increase:

our justice and God's peace.

Huub Oosterhuis

Liturgy of the Eucharist: The Preparation of the Gifts

he second ritual part of the Mass is the eucharist itself: the blessing over the bread and wine, the breaking of the bread, the holy communion. Following the intercessions and before the eucharistic prayer, there are some rather informal moments, moments that are more private and relaxed. Like the opening rites, this is a time of transition. The preparation of the table for the eucharist and the collection are the only tasks of this rite.

We are setting the table. To have some members of the assembly do this says clearly whose table it is, and who provides the bread and wine. This is not the best place for songs about offering, or for any singing at all by the assembly. There might be instrumental or choral music.

The only things placed on the table, other than the altar cloth, are the vessels with the bread and wine and the book. A single container holds enough bread for everyone present; the directives are very clear in stating that the bread for the assembly's communion is to be consecrated at this Mass, not taken from the tabernacle. The vessel should correspond to the kind of container we would expect to hold bread. For the wine, there is a chalice and a glass flagon or other vessel that can hold a quantity sufficient to share with all present. The vessels should make their task obvious: to hold bread, to hold wine. As for the book, if some support is needed, a stand or cushion, this should not be so large as to be distracting. We should avoid placing microphones or other distractions on the table.

If other objects are brought forward as part of the preparation rite, the bread and wine will not be the focal point. Anything that is part of the feast or season could be present from the beginning of the liturgy or could be carried in the entrance procession. This part of the Mass is the preparation of the gifts and table for the eucharist. As with everything else in the liturgy, we are to do what we are doing well—not something else.

Lack of pomp does not mean that there is nothing special surrounding the preparation of the table, but that this specialness is to be found in simple and reverent handling of the vessels containing the bread and wine. The bread, which is unleavened and must be seen and touched, tasted and smelled as "actual food" (*General Instruction*, 283), and the wine inspire this reverence: God's gifts and the work of human hands. Some have expressed fear that if the bread of the eucharist does not seem to be entirely different from everyday forms of bread, people will not hold it in reverence. But Christians make a different point at eucharist: It is precisely in the ordinariness of everyday bread, of food and of communion together, that we meet the Lord. We are to be a people who regard every bit of bread and every person who shares it with reverence. At Mass, the reverence with which the bread and wine are handled may extend to honoring them with incense.

The *General Instruction* notes that this time of preparation "is also the time to receive money or other gifts for the church. These are to be put in a suitable place, but not on the altar" (49). The collecting of money is the work of the ushers, whose manner reflects their basic task of hospitality. Enough ushers should be involved so that the time given to this collection is not out of proportion to other parts of the liturgy. All the members of the assembly should take part in this sharing, including those involved in special ministries. In many parishes, the assembly takes a more active role by coming forward in procession with the gifts of money and goods for the poor.

The preparation time concludes with the presider asking all to pray together about the action we are now to begin. It is fitting that the assembly remain seated until all have answered "Amen" to the prayer over the gifts, which concludes this time of preparation. In this way, the preparation time is clearly separated from the eucharistic prayer by moving to a standing posture.

1. To ready ourselves for any proper meal we need space and time. How do you prepare for a family meal? What are the essentials?

2. While we want to avoid pomp in bringing the gifts to the table, we also want to avoid a casualness that turns the preparation of gifts into a mere relocation of bread and wine from the back of the room to the altar. This is a delicate balance; what goes into making it work?

3. Does an usher or liturgical coordinator appoint people before Mass to carry the gifts to the table so that there is no rush to find gift-bearers at the last minute?

4. Does an usher or coordinator instruct the gift-bearers before Mass in how to hold the vessels, how to walk in procession to the table and how to return to their places in the assembly?

To the total offer that is made me, I can only answer by a total acceptance. I shall therefore react to the eucharistic contact with the entire effort of my life — of my life of today and of my life of tomorrow, of my personal life and of my life as linked to all other lives. Periodically, the sacred species may perhaps fade away in me. But each time they will leave me a little more deeply engulfed in the layers of your omnipresence: Living and dying, I shall never at any moment cease to move forward in you. Thus the precept implicit in your church, that we must communicate everywhere and always, is justified with extraordinary force and precision. The Eucharist must invade my life. My life must become, as a result of the sacrament, an unlimited and endless contact with you — that life which seemed, a few moments ago, like a baptism with you in the waters of the world, now reveals itself to me as communion with you through the world. It is the sacrament of life. The sacrament of my life — of my life received, of my life lived, of my life surrendered.

Pierre Teilhard de Chardin

Liturgy of the Eucharist: The Eucharistic Prayer

ucharist for Christians is a way to grasp what our lives are all about. Eucharist is the praise of God, it is being thank-filled, a way of life rather than an occasional "thank you." True to our roots in Judaism, when this way of living and being is expressed in a word or in a rite, it is blessing God, praising God, over one another, over creation, over events. The rite with which Christians have most identified themselves from their very early years is such a blessing: the praise and thanks given to God over the bread and cup, a rite familiar from the daily and the festive prayer of observant Jews and filled with associations with Jesus.

There are some problems with the way we generally experience the eucharistic prayer today. In form, it usually comes across as a monologue recounting many of our reasons to be thankful including the story of the Last Supper, a monologue occasionally interrupted for a bit of reciting or singing by the assembly. We catch only a dim echo of gathering around the holy table where bread and wine by their beauty and presence evoke memories of Jesus and of all God's love for us, evoke wonder and thanks.

A more serious problem is that the constant giving of praise and thanks does not fill our days, and so we have little to bring to this kind of moment. How do we learn to give the kind of thanks that our faith is about?

At this point in the renewal of our liturgical prayer, we can only begin to acquire some sense of what this ritual is to feel like. This prayer must be the praise and thanks of God by the whole assembly: It is given words by the presider, but in the acclamations there comes a sense of this as the prayer and action of the whole church present. The second Eucharistic Prayer for Masses with Children shows very clearly that acclamations—whether occurring often or limited to the Holy, Holy, memorial acclamation and Amen—are crucial to the experience of the eucharistic prayer as the "center of the entire celebration." In that model, there are five acclamations before the institution narrative when the Last Supper is recalled, two within it

and five after. What has been said of posture, of music and of gesture (in *Environment and Art in Catholic Worship* and in the *Directory for Masses with Children*) applies here. Acclamations are to be sung by heart and with enthusiasm. It is possible that in some settings simple gestures may accompany this singing and give an added dimension of total participation in the great thanksgiving prayer.

The role of the presider is crucial. He is to invite the assembly to prayer: "Lift up your hearts. . . . Let us give thanks to the Lord." With word, posture and gesture, the presider is to make the praise and thanksgiving seen and heard, and so to invite and partake in the acclamations. The assembly does these acclamations, not as little songs here and there, but as joyous ritual affirmations of what is taking place. Over the simple gifts of bread and wine, all, presider and assembly, remember Jesus and all the wonder of creation and liberation. With many different emotions, we remember and give thanks. In its simplicity, the praise and thanksgiving can contain everything.

But often the rite is treated as merely a number of prayers to be said. People are left to follow along in booklets and to read "acclamations." Rather, the assembly needs acclamations to punctuate the prayer at key moments—not unlike cheerleaders who use well-known chants to punctuate and highlight significant moments in a sports event. We need to eliminate patterns of posture and speech that make it seem that the people's part is only to adore and to be spectators. We have much to learn about this central prayer in our liturgy and how to experience it.

There are ten eucharistic prayers now for use in the United States. Among them, they give some sense of what may vary and what is fairly consistent in the wording and shaping of this rite. And together, also, they give that sense that what is being done may be worded in a number of ways, but the words are always to help express the praise and thanks to God who has brought the people here.

1. How can we set for ourselves the goal of doing the eucharistic prayer in a way that makes it an expression of praise and thanksgiving for all—week after week?

2. What in your experience makes for a prayerful rendering of the eucharistic prayer?

3. Some people hesitate to suggest a sung eucharistic prayer because it might take too much time. Experiment by timing a carefully read eucharistic prayer and one that is sung.

4. How can your parish assure the use of all the approved eucharistic prayers through the course of the year? Invite the parish liturgy committee to watch the LTP video "Lift Up Your Hearts" and discuss implications for the parish.

The earliest posture that was assumed by Christians during the eucharistic prayer was standing with outstretched arms *(orans).*

From the eighth to the thirteenth centuries, those fully participating at a liturgy continued to stand for all presidential prayers, including the Canon. Rather than outstretched arms, however, participants stood with heads bowed *(inclinans);* the presider alone stood upright with outstretched arms.

The piety of the thirteenth century brought about a major change. The faithful were admonished to kneel whenever they saw "the Lord's Body." Officially, however, the posture of the assembly continued to be determined by the level of its participation which, in turn, was determined by the rank of the celebration: For Sundays and feasts, at *missa solemnia* or *missa cantata,* full participants were to stand except for the elevation; for penitential days, at *missa privata* or *missa lecta,* those "in attendance" were to kneel throughout except for the gospel.

For a variety of reasons, the *missa lecta* or Low Mass became the norm even on Sundays and feastdays. Even when the *missa cantata* or *missa solemnia* was celebrated, most assemblies continued to assume the postures of the Low Mass.

Vatican II called for a revision of the Mass so that the "intrinsic nature of its several parts, as well as the connection between them, may be more clearly manifested, and that devout and active participation by the faithful may be more easily achieved."

The church is still in the process of heeding that call.

Nathan Mitchell and John Leonard

Liturgy of the Eucharist: The Breaking of the Bread

fter the great Amen, there is a change of tone. The eucharistic prayer, which has a unity from the preface dialogue to the Amen, is over. Now there are several brief rites surrounding the eating of the bread and drinking from the cup: the Lord's Prayer, the peace, the breaking of the bread. A pause (during which the ministers of communion might join the presider at the altar) may separate the Amen from the Lord's Prayer. This is a chance to take a deep breath.

The *General Instruction* notes the tradition of the Lord's Prayer at this time in the liturgy: "This is a petition both for daily food, which is provided for Christians especially in the body of Christ, and for forgiveness from sin, so that what is holy may be given to those who are prepared" (56). The Our Father has familiar words and is for everyone. Singing it may strengthen the bond that is felt in this prayer as long as everyone present feels confident in singing. As Robert Hovda wrote, "The entire communion rite is one of peace, solidarity, unity. These virtues and sentiments indicate the special emphasis of the communion rite and the theme that should be dominant in this part of the service. So the prayer of Jesus, at its beginning, with its articulation of our common sisterhood and brotherhood before God and our willingness to forgive one another, invites a vivid expression of oneness."

There is little left of the resistance with which some reacted when the peace greeting was brought back to the liturgy. It is an ancient gesture among Christians, this physical embrace within the liturgy. The peace greeting is not a social occasion within the liturgy, not a time for visiting and exchanging news. Parish catechesis may be useful here. The greeting is a ritual, and it should be strong enough in its expression to convey a deep and honest sense of our bonds as church. Ushers make sure that any strangers are offered the peace of the community. All in all, the peace greeting makes our vision of the reign of God a little more tangible. To quote Robert Hovda again, "We don't have to go to church to embrace, but the church embrace is one of total, intentional and sacred mystery. Our eyes are opened to the depths of personal being—a situation in which obvious behavior, good or bad, no longer dominates our response to that person."

The next moment in the rite is intimately bound to the peace which goes before and to the communion which follows. It is the breaking of the bread, the rite which in the early church named the whole ritual: They met for "the breaking of the bread." Who can say what the breaking of the bread means? It is something visible, bread being pulled apart, broken. This wordless breaking came from the family table and the meals of friends. It somehow expressed how Christians understood themselves. The gesture never disappeared, even during the centuries when communion was likely to be taken only by the priest. Today the *General Instruction* insists that we use altar bread that can be broken and distributed. We need to pay attention to how we celebrate this simple but powerful rite. We can begin by using more substantial portions of bread. Simple recipes are available for parishioners who are willing to assume responsibility for baking the unleavened eucharistic bread. The amount of bread to be used for a particular liturgy is easily judged with experience. The same is true for the wine.

Now that the bread has been broken, additional plates and cups are brought to the table. Until now, there would have been only a single plate or basket, a single cup and one large container for wine. Now the bread is broken or distributed into the smaller plates; the wine is poured into the cups. Only if there has been some miscalculation in planning for the amount of bread needed should anyone take previously consecrated bread from the tabernacle. Using consecrated bread from the tabernacle is strongly discouraged in the *General Instruction* (56).

When we offer the cup to all who come forward, we give full strength to the symbol which is fruit of the vine and work of human hands, a human expression of delight, festivity and communion. In the eucharistic liturgy, the sharing of the cup brings all this into our far richer sharing in the covenant. Regular catechesis on the meaning of the eucharistic cup will assure regular sharing of the cup as the normal manner of parish eucharist.

The preparation for communion is carried out with directness, but with great reverence and respect for the consecrated bread and wine and for the assembly. The deacon and ministers of communion assist the presider in preparing the plates and cups. During this time, the cantor leads the assembly in another litany, the Lamb of God. The refrain "Have mercy on us" is to be sung over and over again until all the communion plates and cups are prepared, and then the final response is sung: "Grant us peace."

1. In your parish, is there anything standing in the way of the full opening-up of the symbols in the eucharistic prayer, the peace, the breaking of the bread? What? How can it be removed?

2. Discuss how the cup is offered without undue delay in the liturgy. How many ministers of communion are needed?

3. Has the liturgy committee read and discussed the book *The Communion Rite at Sunday Mass* as found in the bibliography?

The body of Christ that is the Eucharist is not
a private party, a me and Jesus two-step.
The body of Christ that is the Eucharist
makes the Body of Christ that is the Church.
It is broken not to satisfy isolated individuals
but to build community. It is broken
particularly for those who are themselves
uncommonly broken, who share
more of Jesus' crucifixion than
of his resurrection. That body is broken
and given even for those who have not
the joy of receiving it.

Walter Burghardt, SJ

There is another expectation for those who truly have
come to recognize the Lord Jesus in the breaking
of the bread and who have been fed with the eucharistic
food: The divine love which is a fruit of this sacrament
must make it ever more possible to find and
recognize Christ in every single human being, especially
in those human beings whom he calls "the least
of his brothers and sisters" (see Mt. 25.31 – 46).
When he comes in glory at the end of time...he will
ask us whether we recognized and served him
in the hungry and the thirsty, the stranger and the
naked, the sick and the imprisoned, in short, in every
single human being who is deprived in one way
or another of full human rights and dignity.

Bishop Donald Trautman

Liturgy of the Eucharist: Communion

mmediately after the breaking of the bread, the presider invites the assembly to share in holy communion. This invitation may be worded in the customary way, or may incorporate other words from scripture or tradition. But the invitation must be beyond words: in the tone of voice, the eyes, the posture and gesture. This is why the presider holds out the plate and the cup as he speaks. Once the invitation is given, the communion begins. There should be no great division here, either in time or in the manner of communion, between the presider's communion, that of the other ministers and that of the rest of the assembly. Often the best arrangement is for the ministers to receive communion after the assembly.

We have ministers to assist the presider because the eating and drinking are a "communion:" Unity is what they are all about. As much as possible, we are to be at table together; a family meal or formal banquet, not a cafeteria, should be our model. As communion from the cup is restored at Sunday Mass, additional ministers are needed so that holy communion feels like eating and drinking together.

The manner of coming forward can itself speak clearly about the sharing. It should be neither a military drill organized by the ushers, nor a random lining-up organized by no one but dominated by the swiftest. This is to be a procession in the full, communal sense. We sing at this time to give clear expression to our communion, our unity together in Christ. Thus, the assembly's part should be simple antiphons and refrains, nothing that would require a book or song sheet. Even posture is a sign of common sharing. The practice of communion in the hand suggests that one hand be cupped within the other to receive communion. Perhaps the hands could be held in this posture throughout the procession if people are uncomfortable with folding their hands in the traditional way. However one holds one's hands, a totally casual posture is painfully out of place.

In many places it is common for the minister of communion to place a hand on the head of children who have not yet begun to receive communion. This simple gesture, with or without a word of greeting or blessing, speaks well of what holy communion is about.

In presenting the bread or cup, it is essential that there be a personal moment, a meeting of eyes when one says "The body of Christ," "The blood of Christ," and the other affirms "Amen." Then the bread or cup is given from one person to another. Nothing automatic or impersonal belongs in the word or gesture of either person. The entire communion rite should say clearly that the people are a "holy communion," pledged together to a holy life.

After the eating and drinking, the plates and cups are returned quietly to a side table. The altar is empty again. The washing of the vessels may be done after the liturgy so that now there can be quiet and stillness, no one moving around, for a little while. Everyone is seated. Lighting may be turned down. Music, instrumental or choral, may sometimes serve this meditation time. A generous space of time is needed, with consistency from week to week. This silent time too is an expression of communion. Habits of prayer need to be formed.

The communion rite, and the liturgy of the eucharist, concludes with the prayer after communion. The silence leads into this. It is a simple, short prayer giving voice to our desire that what we have just done together will have continued results in our lives.

1. We have objectified so much in our way of living. This attitude inhabits our economic cathedrals and our temples of worship. We can even objectify the eucharist into mere bread and wine. But eucharist is not a thing. It is sharing, a breaking of bread, a sharing of the cup: an action. What can we do to increase our awareness of eucharist as our common deed?

2. The assembly is most personally involved at liturgy in the sharing of the bread and cup. How do the eucharistic ministers make the moment of communion a treasured moment of grace?

3. What actions convey a sense of reverence and love?

If, then, you wish to understand the body of Christ, listen to the apostle as he says to the faithful, You are the body of Christ, and his members, your mystery has been placed on the Lord's table, you receive your mystery. You reply "Amen" to that which you are, and by replying you consent. For you hear "The body of Christ," and you reply "Amen." Be a member of the body of Christ so that your "Amen" may be true.

Saint Augustine

And to be hospitable in every liturgical act is crucial. When you offer the cup in particular I think you really need to give it to people in a way that they know that it belongs to them. It doesn't belong to me. It belongs to all of us and to share it. So I really try to reach up to them with the cup. And if I don't even think they're going to take it, I give it to them. I make sure that they have it in their hands. I don't at all want to withhold the cup. And with children in particular I try to give it to them and often will say "Take the cup."

Christina Neff

Concluding Rites

This is again a time of transition: from the prayer together to our individual lives. When the prayer after communion is finished, there is a sense of conclusion. It is a leave-taking rite. When friends part, they have rituals: a hug, a wave, some spoken formula, "Take care," "See you soon." These are comfortable ways to get through the parting, familiar ways to express ourselves. Large groups have rituals for the same purpose: the formal voting to adjourn, or curtain calls at the end of a theatrical performance. Such moments mix the formal and informal, and contain much of what the whole time together was about.

At the end of the Mass, the leave-taking rite usually consists of announcements, the blessing, the dismissal, a song and procession. It is important to see these together, and to see them in light of their purpose: an ending that leaves good feelings about what has happened here and an eagerness to assemble again. If the liturgy has been good prayer together, then the closing has something bittersweet about it. Hurrying through it, letting it become just one set of words after another so that announcements and blessing and dismissals blur together, diminishes the rite.

The announcements are to be brief. They are like the welcome before the liturgy began, part of the hospitality: sharing information about the community in an informal and friendly manner. They are not best done by the presider (since he has just spoken the prayer after communion and will next do the blessing) but by the one who offered the first words of welcome or by one who naturally represents the day-to-day work of this church. The last announcement invites all into the singing of the closing song, if there is to be one.

The blessing is the heart of the concluding rite. Many forms for this are now provided, all building toward the final "May almighty God bless you..." Or that form may stand by itself. There is also the gesture: outstretched hands during the three-part blessing, with bowing of heads, and the sign of the cross during the final words. The assembly responds with "Amen" to the three-part blessings when these are used. These Amens need to be habitual and strong, not awkward mumblings. The cadence of the sung or spoken words of blessing can do much to bring forth a good Amen. The words of various blessings, if some of them are used consistently, may provide forms for blessings apart from the Mass: the blessing of children at night, of one another before a journey, of the sick.

The dismissal is given by the deacon, as are many of the practical instructions for the assembly throughout the liturgy. The words can vary, but should always make it easy and comfortable for people to respond together, "Thanks be to God." The strength of the words and manner of the speaker, along with a consistent and obvious conclusion, will let that final response of the assembly be loud and firm.

What follows has no prescribed format. In most places, there is a hymn and a procession of the ministers through the assembly. That is one approach. Another would be to let the sung blessing, with a strong "Amen" response, feel like a conclusion, and then the dismissal is just that: Leaving and visiting begin at once, perhaps with some organ or other instrumental music. Or the conclusion may somehow be tied to the entrance rites, as the Gregorian chant did when the "Ite Missa est" was sung to the same melody as the "Kyrie." This could be done during the seasons, thus echoing the mood set in the entrance rite, reinforcing it as a mood to be taken home. For this, songs from the entrance rite could be repeated, or silence, when appropriate, could accompany the procession of the ministers. The ministers, especially the ushers, are still responsible for hospitality. This may be in visiting or in a goodbye and a smile while handing out bulletins. This last impression may be remembered longest.

1. Our rites have conclusions. We care about how we end one thing and so begin something new. How do we express this care at wedding receptions, burials, retirement parties, school graduations, birthdays? Does our conclusion at eucharist deserve any less care? What new beginnings does this usher in?

2. When are the announcements done—within the communion rite (before the prayer after communion) or as part of the conclusion? How are they done?

3. How does the mood change from the time after communion to the moments of the blessing and dismissal?

The community the celebrates the Eucharist in prospect of the kingdom must ask itself whether its table sharing in the Eucharist is reflected in a just sharing of the gifts of the earth or whether some are deprived of the means of life because others hoard the world's goods for their own advantage. Eucharistic participation must lead first of all to a new social vision, then to a critique of our existing society in the light of that vision, and finally to advocacy for the poor and disadvantaged members of society and to social change. The community gathered around the table of the Lord must be prepared to have its entire common life in the world placed under both judgment and grace.

William R. Crockett

❖

Our problem is how to live what we pray, how to make our lives a daily commentary on our prayer book, how to live in consonance with what we promise, how to keep faith with the vision we pronounce.

Abraham Joshua Heschel

Days and Seasons

A bird's-eye view of the church year can make it seem quite complex, with its seasons of joy and anticipation; its Sundays, holy days, feasts days and solemnities; its colored clothes and decorations.

In this unit you will find an introduction to each of the elements of the church year in order to discover something of the mood or spirit that each season calls forth from us. The introductions will help you appreciate the scriptures that are proclaimed in the Sunday assembly during the seasons of the year, the songs that you sing and the prayers that you pray. The seasons and festivals of the church year are basic to planning liturgy, and to the way home and parish together shape our prayer and our lives.

Naming the Days

n all our different groups, we name certain days. Citizens of the United States name Independence Day. Music lovers name Beethoven's birthday. Irish-Americans name Saint Patrick's Day. Couples name anniversaries. We scatter such special days among the ordinary ones, giving the year a rhythm of anticipation: "How many days is it until…?" Some of our special days grow beyond 24 hours and become a whole season: a short one like Thanksgiving weekend or a long one like the weeks before Christmas.

The days we have named are meant to be kept. We *keep* days (as in "How are you keeping Lent this year?" or "Remember to keep holy the Sabbath day") by holding to them, remembering them and letting them stir memories in us, as a wedding anniversary or the Fourth of July is supposed to do. We keep them by letting the memories lead to observances, the little rites of word or deed with which we mark the day: birthday cake, firecrackers, Halloween costumes. We keep the days—*and the days keep us!* That happens with the wedding anniversary: We remember the day, we fill it with specialness, and it tells us who we are, keeps us who we are. Or we keep the Fourth of July with parades, song, music, gatherings outdoors, fireworks—and doing that re-creates us as something more like a free people. Or, in the recent past (and perhaps again now), we Catholics kept Fridays by not eating meat. Somehow our solidarity in this kept us, gave us a sense of belonging within a church, identified us to ourselves and to others.

That kind of community is basically what the naming and keeping of days and seasons is all about. These are ways that go beyond textbooks, beyond statements of creed, beyond even common convictions about morality: They gather this and all else in life together in ways that make it all very personal and yet shared. Seasons and days that we name let us take all that it is to be Christian and express it in songs, in stories, in dances, in colors and textures and much more. To do this, and do it over and over through the years, is the way a people hands on faith from generation to generation. It can happen only within a people, not in the abstract. The stories we tell and all the other

rites of the seasons are open enough, ambiguous enough, to remain strong year after year.

That is the point. They are my story, our stories. They are about me, my life, about us, our life together as church. And so with the songs and other rites of each season: Their strength lies in the way they are not simply pieces of data somewhere out there which the individual is to approach, study and perhaps adapt to. Rather, they are inside us, and the task of those who would help create an Advent or an All Saints Day is to be in touch with what it is inside every person that is being called forth in this particular day or season. The feasts and the seasons are not gimmicks, hooks for stories of the lives of Jesus and the saints. We need to name our days and to keep them: They help us remember who we are and what it is to be the church.

The first day we name is Sunday. We keep this day with Mass together, and in other ways, to make it a "kingdom" day, a day of new creation and of freedom from slavery and sin and death. Sunday is called the eighth day, the day beyond our cycle of time. It is called the Lord's day; thus it stands first in our calendar, marking the rhythm of our lives with the proclamation of the word and the breaking of the bread.

Many Sundays fall within our seasons of Advent, Christmastime, Lent and Eastertime, and at these times the Sunday liturgy takes on the mood and spirit of that season. These seasons are larger than their Sundays, however, and seek ways to be kept beyond the eucharistic liturgy. A season has its own spirit: We seek this spirit in words and stories that catch something of it, or in various sounds that bring it to us, or in ways of moving, or in all sorts of uses of color and materials. We never really pin that spirit down, saying that Advent means precisely this or that. We can only deal with it in words of poetry, for it is too close to us for anything else.

The work of the liturgy expresses something of this spirit in ways that can bring the Advent or the Lent out in people, more each year, until the keeping of the seasons tells us we belong here.

1. The keeping of holidays, feasts and seasons helps us maintain a necessary rhythm and vitality in our lives. We need these special days to lift us out of the ordinariness of everyday. Holidays, feasts and seasons are not for producing things or accomplishing goals. They are days to enjoy, to remember, to be in touch with our history, our relationships, our tradition of faith. They point to a deeper and more profound sense of who we are and where we are going: not in an intellectual or academic manner, but in a way that allows our entire selves to celebrate. What days do this for you? How?

2. "Keeping the day"—this phrase seems to give freedom and belonging! What day will you name and keep within the next few months? What rituals of anticipation will you perform? Have others kept this day before you? How long is the "day"? Twenty-four hours? A week? What stories will surround the naming?

3. What days are really special in your parish?

4. What do we do besides use the sacramentary's proper prayers to commemorate a feast or keep a season?

5. Think of a feast day celebration you greatly enjoyed. What made it so?

Christ's saving work is celebrated

in sacred memory by the Church

on fixed days throughout the year.

Each week on the day called

the Lord's Day the Church commemorates

the Lord's resurrection. Once a year

at Easter the Church honors the resurrection

and passion with the utmost solemnity.

In fact through the yearly cycle the Church

unfolds the entire mystery of Christ

and keeps the anniversaries of the saints.

During the different seasons of

the liturgical year, the Church, in accord

with traditional discipline, carries out

the formation of the faithful by means of

devotional practices, both interior

and exterior, instruction, and works

of penance and mercy.

General Norms for the Liturgical Year and Calendar, *1*

Advent

t has long been common for peoples to surround the shortest, darkest and coldest days of the year with special ritual. This has often had in it something of both fear and promise. For some, that was simple fear of the dark and cold: realities we have found ways to avoid, though we still fear them. And it was fear that the precious food supply might not last until the time of planting and growth and harvest. The hope that came through in the darkest days of winter was often seen in the sun, which at last ended its decline and began to stay just a bit longer, rise a bit higher, each day, pledging better days ahead. Christians, in placing festivals of the birthday of Jesus and his manifestation around the winter solstice, were doing what came naturally. The anticipation and celebration of those events, birth and manifestation, were our way to talk of what fear and promise meant in the church.

But more than just talk. The days that came to be known as Advent were never meant only to teach something about Christ's coming in past, present and future. They are expressions of the advent inside each of us. Part of that is the fears we have, all of them. They are not attached to any particular time of year, our fears, but being afraid is just as much a part of the human condition as it ever was, maybe more. There are private, family, community fears. Somehow, then, what we do in Advent—the stories we tell, songs we sing, customs we observe—lets us admit to those fears. More than this, the keeping of Advent meets that fear with a promise—not in some historical sense of foretelling the coming of Jesus who has now come, but in the sense that being the church is a response to God's promise and is somehow itself a promise to one another and to the Lord.

And that, perhaps, says a little about the feeling that these days before Christmas have. But a more effective way to enter into Advent, to feel at home here, is to seek it out inside us and inside Advent's texts and music and colors. A good beginning may be to search through the scriptures of Advent's Sundays and weekdays. What are the key words, words that open up the mood? Every list will be different,

but here is an example: leap, sing, be with child, bloom, stay awake, steady, await, kiss, bring forth, stand up straight, filled, made low, be strong, be opened, be cleared, burn, spring, look down, withered, vanish, sway, climb, clear, rescue, walk, look forward, overshadow.

These are strong images. How do they express themselves? In phrases from "O come, O come, Emmanuel" or from "Wake, awake," or from the "O" antiphons? Or what do such images sound like—not only in church music but in popular music, or classical or folk or rock or jazz? Each type of music must sometimes express the advent that is in the composer or performer. Or, what musical instruments sound like these images? Or, what stories do such images point to?—stories from scripture, yes, but also stories from the newspapers, from novels, from the movies? What characters seem to have something like Advent about them?

If Advent has its words, its music (and other sounds too) and its stories, it also has its colors (and not just purple), its textures, its designs. Do the colors blend or are they in sharp contrast during Advent? And it even has its tastes: Is Advent sour, sweet, bitter, sweet and sour, bland, salty, rich? People may name these differently, which is natural, but in discussing these there will be overlapping and building to show what sense we may already have of this season.

We Christians don't often discuss together the longings, the waitings, the darkness we feel deep within ourselves. Perhaps we judge that these feelings are uniquely our own or else just not the kind of thing to be shared. But they are our common ground for celebrating Advent. Ultimately, all the longing and waiting in our lives leads toward the Lord.

During the weeks of Advent, liturgy is to let that longing and waiting shape our prayer. With great simplicity so that the words may be heard, the music felt and the colors seen, and with consistency from week to week, Advent is brought out and takes shape in the community. Words and tunes and colors and stories are all woven together into a whole, a time we can come home to year after year.

1. Search the scriptures and music of Advent and let the words rise to meet you. Make your list of strong words and phrases. Spend time in meditation and in sharing your lists.

2. What has been the mood of Advent in your life? How does that match the parish celebration of Advent? What kind of wine for the eucharist would help us in our Advent awareness?

3. What would we lose if we eliminated Advent from our calendar?

4. How do we preserve a sense of Advent in parish homes in the rush of Christmas parties and shopping?

The Pilgrim Way has led to the Abyss.

Was it to meet such grinning evidence

We left our richly odoured ignorance?

Was the triumphant answer to be this?

The Pilgrim Way has led to the Abyss.

We who must die demand a miracle.

How could the Eternal do a temporal act,

The Infinite become a finite fact?

Nothing can save us that is possible:

We who must die demand a miracle.

W. H. Auden

❖

This then is to watch:

to be detached from what is present, and

to live in what is unseen;

To live in the thought of Christ as he came once,

and as he will come again;

to desire his second coming, from our affectionate

and grateful remembrance of his first.

John Henry Newman

Christmastime

ehind the heartbeat of these Christmas days is birth. More than birth, of course. Word-made-flesh. But before we can consider that we have to ponder birth itself. Before we marvel at the incarnation, we must stop to realize that it is marvelous that *any* new person bursts forth and, with the cord cut, cries a very personal cry.

Births fill our folklore. Even our ancestors, who lived closer to such things that we do, never could get over what a wonderful thing it is, this event that links generations, that changes most everything, that at once promises us a future and sentences us to the past. For the delight always has just a bit of fear: The new always does that to human beings and their societies. Herod acts out the part of us that sees in every birth our own death coming closer. Perhaps the mystery and awe and song inspired by birth would not be so great without this darker side.

Stories of marvelous births fill our fairy tales, our myths, our stories from the Hebrew Scriptures; Sarah's laugh resounds through a thousand birth stories of all peoples. It may be the something-more-than-meets-the-eye element in the birth of Jesus, the incarnation then, that makes December 25 just the right date. Birth, after all, is normally an event of springtime, so that the newborn can grow strong before the cold and hunger come again. But this is something else: A birth in midwinter, born with the weak sun.

The first thing liturgy is to do is let this story overtake us. It is a "once upon a time" story, the kind that is more true than facts. There is something in us that thrills to hear of a birth and is absolutely convinced that the only reason things hold together is because God is all mixed up in our clay. Only when we are thus swept off our feet do we know that the Christmas prayer that springs from this story doesn't begin in explanations or theology as such, but in all those human arts that touch the story and open its myriad wonders.

Christmas as a season may seem to be a lost cause. What energy could possibly be left after the American pre-Christmas season? Yet there is still enough festivity called forth by the telling of the story of this birth to carry us through New Year's and to Epiphany. We compete with the world already when we decide to wait through Advent, when we say that you can't hear the story in all its awesomeness, you can't sing the Christmas songs and wear the Christmas colors and make a festival of it — unless you wait. Once that is done, extending the festival through the season is easy. Ordinarily there are five times to gather during the season: Christmas itself, Holy Family, New Year's, Epiphany, the Lord's baptism. The shape of the liturgy on these days can have a certain consistency while scriptures and homily give each its special note.

Local traditions may carry certain aspects of Christmas day itself: where the crèche is placed and how, who sings the Midnight Mass, where the flowers go. Hospitality may flourish for some of the Christmas Day Masses as at no other time of the year. Anything worth so much effort is worth savoring in the days that follow. Some of the sounds can be sustained through Epiphany, some of the flowers, some of the special scents of many candles and of incense. Images evolve within this time, dwelling on one after another of the moments in the stories of birth and manifestation. In the twelve days of Christmas and in various ethnic customs associated with the season, customs attached to Epiphany as much as Christmas, we sense possibilities. The celebration is poetic, not bound to literal understandings of the sequence of events, but dancing around, mixing up, touching on what's just beyond the rational. Manger and magi and gifts of gold are all mixed up with water turned to wine and Jesus deep in the Jordan beside John. No one can really explain what's going on here — and you don't have to.

1. A start for a Christmas list of words from liturgy and culture: birth, gift, bells, light in darkness, lightheartedness, the unexpected, stars in sky and eyes, stories, manifestations. Carry it on!

2. Christmas is a homecoming feast. Old parishioners, college students and infrequent worshipers come home to celebrate Christmas. How can all these homecomers be made to feel welcome?

3. Some parishes plan very fine celebrations for Christmas day, but then let Holy Family, Mary, Mother of God and Epiphany slip away without much observance. How can all these days be woven together into one joyous holiday?

For a Christian there is nothing peculiarly difficult about Christmas in a prison cell. I daresay it will have more meaning and be observed with greater sincerity here in this prison than in places where all that survives of the feast is its name. The misery, suffering, poverty, loneliness, helplessness and guilt look very different to the eyes of God from what they do to man, that God should come down to the very place where men usually abhor, that Christ was born in a stable because there was no room for him in the inn — these are things which prisoners can understand better than anyone else. For the prisoner the Christmas story is glad tidings in a very real sense. And that faith gives a prisoner a part in the communion of saints, a fellowship transcending the bounds of time and space and reducing the months of confinement here to insignificance.

Dietrich Bonhoeffer

It is an *adult* Christ that the community encounters during the Advent and Christmas cycles of Sundays and feasts: a Risen Lord who invites sinful people to become the church. Christmas does not ask us to pretend we were back in Bethlehem, kneeling before a crib; it asks us to recognize that the wood of the crib became the wood of the cross.

Nathan Mitchell

Lent

he season of Lent developed as days of preparation for Easter and, more precisely, as days of preparation for the Easter initiation of catechumens into the fullness of the community. Over time the keeping of forty days became the common practice, and the entire community entered into the season with those about to be initiated and with those who were returning to the faith. Even if there were no catechumens preparing for baptism, Lent remained a season turned toward the renewal of baptism: inviting all to hear the gospel well, to take it in with great seriousness, to experience something of the dying and rising that baptized life is all about.

Lent is an intense time. It begins with a stark action that continue to speak to people: the marking with ashes. Ashes, in the time of year when things are yet bleak, image what is common to all the living: the end of everything, the beginning of everything. On this Wednesday, while life bustles on, Christians are marked with ashes by ministers who are themselves marked with ashes. The ashes call into question all that bustling life, all ourselves. There is something here that speaks of working through pretenses and getting to the real, of facades that crumble, of what our lives are like through these forty days. The liturgy of Ash Wednesday centers on the marking with blessed ashes: This is accompanied by scriptures as well as psalms and other singing of the day.

The Sunday scriptures of Lent, especially those in Year A, build one on the other. The gospel readings can be viewed together as a lenten gospel, a story told by this season as a whole. As always, it is about us; it is our story, as individuals and as church. The gospels can be a beginning point in discovering the shape of the liturgy during these weeks. What does Lent sound like? What are the rhythms, what is the volume, what is the tempo? What is the pace? Where is the silence? Similar questions must be put to every other art that serves the liturgy. How does the whole sustain and encourage the keeping of Lent in the home and the individual's life?

More and more, Lent in the parish is marked by the presence of the catechumens during the liturgy of the word, by the rites of their election (the final step of preparation before baptism), and by the special prayers on some

Sundays of Lent that witness to the nearness of that baptism. In these rites, the catechumens are present only until the time of preparation for the eucharist, when they leave, usually to gather in another place for prayer and reflection on the scriptures. This is a powerful sign of what initiation into the church means: joining the baptized in doing eucharist and sharing holy communion. The presence of a group of catechumens in the midst of the church during Lent is the greatest help in renewing this season. Could there be a better witness to the baptized of the faith they profess? What else could state so strongly what it means to be church? The presence of those who seek full belonging leads those who already belong into a thoughtfully-kept Lent.

The Sunday liturgies of Lent need consistency in song and color and pace to tie all six weeks together. These constants make clear, without anyone having to verbalize it, "This is Lent, our Lent." This comes through in the way the preparation rite is handled: how it differs from Ordinary Time and other seasons not just in the obvious, that is, in the words of the songs, but in the use of silence, in the choice of instruments for the procession music, in the length and solemnity of the penitential rite. Lent is also made clear in the use of an appropriate refrain for the responsorial psalm, one that is kept all through Lent; in the special gospel acclamation; in the form of the final blessing; in the way the dismissal is handled; in the use of fewer colors in the room and in the absence of unnecessary furniture; in dramatic presentations of Lent's scriptures. When the whole season has this kind of unity, allowing the rites to become familiar to everyone, then the things that are unique to each week — scriptures, the scrutinies of the candidates for baptism — these have a well-prepared place to do their work.

Lent does not stay at the altar: It fills the parish. It is in our homes and our own personal ways of thinking and doing things. This takes everyone's cooperation. It presumes some communal and personal disciplines. It means we might have to let go of some things that ordinarily take up our time, so that we are free to welcome candidates for baptism and reception into full communion, and to renew our own baptismal vocation.

1. The lenten sacramentary and lectionary offer us the church's avenue of spiritual direction to lead us into the depths of the paschal mystery to discover what it means to be baptized in Christ, to be rid of sin, to belong to the church. Anything that divides our attention would only weaken our Lent. What are the ways your parish responds to this?

2. Does the parish follow the lenten suggestions in *Sourcebook for Sundays and Seasons?* How?

3. Does the environment change noticeably, even down to a detail like the dry taste of the eucharistic wine?

4. Why do you suppose so many people come to church on the first day of Lent for ashes?

5. What are some of your recollections of Lent in the past? How did these experiences of Lent define the season for you? What can these memories teach us about the present?

6. What powerful disciplines of Lent do we have today? What makes them powerful?

Lent is not tidy. Days grow longer (the word "Lent" comes from "lengthen"), the ground thaws, and the next thing we know, everything is filthy. Our windows need washing, our temples need cleansing, the earth itself needs a good bath. The English names for these months come from ancient words that reflect the need to roll up our sleeves this season: February ("purification") and March ("the spirit of war"). Good names. Winter doesn't leave without blustery battles that push things over and mess things up and even break things. Lent, if we honestly face its fury, will leave the landscape littered with bits and pieces of ourselves.

Sometimes the only antidote is to take more of the poison. And so on our foreheads we rub dirt: Eden gone to ashes, the dustbin emptied of a winter's worth of soot, last years leaves riddled with worms, the broken earth turned by the plow, the dry earth thirsty for water to make it clay of a new creation. And when Lent is done and the Passover arrives we'll have water in abundance, water to bathe our feet and water to drown the demons and water to wash away the winter. And, as Bishop Ambrose reminds us, even if we forget to fill the font, there'll be water in abundance in our tears.

Peter Mazar

The Triduum

he word *Triduum*, three days, refers to the time from the evening liturgy on Holy Thursday until evening prayer on Easter Sunday. The sacramentary says: "The Easter triduum of the passion and resurrection of Christ is thus the culmination of the entire liturgical year. What Sunday is to the week, the solemnity of Easter is to the liturgical year. The Easter triduum begins with the evening Mass of the Lord's Supper, reaches its high point in the Easter vigil, and closes with evening prayer on Easter Sunday." The emphasis is on the unity of the days, on not separating death from resurrection. From its first years, the church has never spoken of one without the other. Triduum is a single celebration.

This means that presentations of Holy Thursday, Good Friday and Holy Saturday that re-enact Jesus' last hours, death and burial are not accurate. Rather, the liturgies of these days make it clear that to speak of Jesus' death is to speak of his resurrection. The Triduum provides the occasion for the most crucial gestures in the initiation of new Christians: fasting, prayer, baptism and confirmation and eucharist. The Triduum is kept as an annual Passover for the whole community, all of those whose existence is defined by those same sacraments. The church keeps the Triduum.

The bond between the Jewish Passover and the Christian sacramental experience of dying and rising with Christ is not simply that the gospels tell us it was at the time of Passover that Jesus was executed and rose from the dead. Rather, the early Jewish followers of Jesus gathered from their own keeping of Passover the notions, words, experiences to name what had happened to Jesus and to them. It was the Passover festival understood as present reality (". . . not for our ancestors only did he do this, but for us . . ."), that made what Jesus did understandable as a present reality in the church. It was Passover as memorial and dedication to freedom that gave them a way to talk about what happened in Jesus and now in the church. And it was Passover as "not yet," as longing for the final liberation, that kept the church's Easter human.

The power of the Holy Thursday liturgy is in its unique gestures, which summon us to memories and hopes of what it means to die and rise in Christ. A gesture like the washing of feet can convey in its own special and strong way our calling to do that, our need to have it done to us, the little ways that we die and rise in such washing and being washed. The gestures say what it means to "pass over," to be church. The evening liturgy needs no embellishment.

The keeping of the Triduum from then until the Vigil liturgy are marked by a number of rites and prayers, such as the services of Good Friday, but the most basic is the ritual of fasting. "On Good Friday, and if possible, also on Holy Saturday until the Easter Vigil, the Easter fast is observed everywhere." (*General Norms for the Liturgical Year,* 18) Note that here the norms speak of an Easter fast, not the lenten fast. The Easter fast is the fast of anticipation before the great festival; it is the fast of the baptized and catechumens together before the Easter sacraments. It is not a fast of repentance but a fast of excitement, a fast of reverence and preparation

The Triduum, one solemn commemoration of Christ's death and rising, reaches its high point at the Easter Vigil. The Easter Vigil is addressed in the Orthodox liturgy: "The spotless Passover, the great Passover, the Passover of the faithful, the Passover which opens to us the gates of Paradise, the Passover which sanctifies all the faithful. The Passover joyful, the Passover of the Lord, the Passover all-majestic has shone forth on us! With joy let us embrace one another! O Passover, release from sorrow!" The Easter Vigil is not a mere anniversary of the resurrection, but is the passing over to life in Christ by those being initiated and the renewing of this life in the whole church. Nothing else in the whole year has such richness as the baptizing, confirming and eucharist that tonight bring to a climax Triduum, Lent and the whole long catechumenate.

In the vigiling and the listening to the grandest stories of our scriptures, in the chants and singing, in the lighting of the new fire, in the flowing waters of baptism, in the rich perfume of the anointing with chrism, in the blessing and sharing of bread and cup, and most of all in the people who do these things together, are expressed the whole meaning and belief of the church. On this night we see more clearly than ever the mystery of Christ, dead and rising, not as an abstract theory but as an ongoing saving event that raises up our own brothers and sisters to eternal life.

1. Why do you think the church names the fast on Good Friday and Holy Saturday the "Easter fast"?

2. What are other times of your life when one act unites several days?

3. What are your experiences and memories of Good Friday and Holy Saturday? How is Easter part of those memories?

4. The liturgies for the Triduum are complex. Keep a careful record of plans and materials. It will be useful for next year's planning.

Easter tells us that God has done something. God has. And this action has not merely gently touched the heart of a person here and there, so that they tremble slightly from an ineffable and nameless someone. God has raised the Son from the dead. God has done this — has conquered — not merely in the realm of inwardness, in the realm of thought, but in the realm where we, the glory of the human mind notwithstanding, are most really ourselves: in the actuality of this world, far from all "mere" thoughts and "mere" sentiments. God has conquered in the realm where we experience practically what we are in essence: children of the earth, who die.

Karl Rahner

It is immensely easier to suffer in obedience to human command than to suffer in the freedom of one's own responsible deed. It is immensely easier to suffer with others than to suffer alone. It is immensely easier to suffer openly and honorably than apart and in shame. It is immensely easier to suffer through commitment of the physical life than in the spirit. Christ suffered in freedom, alone, apart and in shame in body and in spirit, and since then many Christians have suffered with him.

Dietrich Bonhoeffer

Eastertime: Fifty Days of Unbounded Joy!

astertime, the earliest distinct season in Christian communities, is hardly noticed today. Even before Lent took shape, there were 50 days of rejoicing after Easter and its baptisms. The calendar reform of Vatican II not only kept Eastertime as a distinct season, but emphasized its importance by changing the way Sundays of the season are named: from Sundays "after Easter" to Sundays "of Easter." But names do not make a festive season happen. A sense of how this season can be our own, how it comes from the heart, what it expresses of human and Christian experience—this begins with a look at its origins.

Both Lent and Eastertime developed from the keeping of Passover, which became for Christians the time to celebrate the sacraments of initiation. Eastertime prolonged the rejoicing. But Passover itself, the memory and the experience of deliverance from slavery, is crucial. For the Jews, this festival was and is kept with rites that tell of the exodus, tell of it in such a way that there is no doubt that God's saving work was in their ancestors' escape from slavery to freedom, and in the life of the people at all times since. What the followers of Jesus understood about him and his teaching was intimately bound up in what Passover had always meant to them.

But there is another step to take. The Jewish festival of Passover had its roots in the springtime festivals of farmers and shepherds, festivals that rejoiced in the end of winter and the promise of life: life in the warm earth and the rain that would grow the crops, life in the new lambs being born. The community would go on. It was a matter of life and death and this year, it was life! That was cause to rejoice, to give thanks. The life-and-death tale of the Hebrews, death in slavery and life in the escape to freedom, came to be told during these spring festivals. The symbols worked together: the bread and the lamb of the farmers and shepherds resonated with the story of how the people of Israel were saved and how they had to go in haste. The stories and the rites evolved, and their origins were often forgotten, but springtime and the triumph of life and freedom in God's saving work were always celebrated.

So Easter tells a human story, perhaps the most basic of human stories. The world has echoed it in fairy tales and motion pictures. In little ways, the story tells itself in each human life. As Christians, all the stories we tell of exodus and of Jesus and of dry bones and of Abraham and Isaac and Jonah reflect what we believe about the struggle of life and death that forever grips the world and each of us. That story, and what we as church affirm as our experience, is what makes Eastertime.

We shape the Sunday liturgies during Eastertide with many songs and sights, the best we have. There is the simple and beautiful presence of water: the font, the holy water, the rite of sprinkling in the preparation rite for Sunday Mass. There is the Easter candle, large and beautifully crafted and burning during all the liturgies of the season. There is extra light and color everywhere! There is the sound of our alleluias, sung to melodies that are used only during these days, and the strong hymns of Eastertime. Overall, the Eastertime liturgies might be known for their feeling of peace, of gentleness, of the powerful silence in which the seed sprouts, the bud swells, the tomb becomes womb. This quiet joy permeates all the gospels of the Easter weeks: Jesus and Mary in the garden, the upper room, the stranger cooking breakfast, the Emmaus supper, the discourse from John's gospel. Every art used in liturgy serves this spirit, shaping a way for the church to pray in these weeks, a way that can be repeated year after year. As in every season, we seek the ways to express the spirit of the season in sounds, colors, textures, tastes, melodies, movements. A beautiful and resonant Eastertime invites us to celebrate with the fullness of our deeply Christian voices and eyes and hands.

For the early church, the 50 days after Easter formed the period of mystagogia. This is a time to plunge more deeply into the Easter mysteries, drawing on the experience of these mysteries in the Easter sacraments. The church believed that only after experiencing baptism could the newly initiated really understand the mysteries. Baptism was illumination: Eyes were opened. The community shared these Eastertime gatherings with the newly initiated and all reflected together on Christ's presence within their community.

Eastertime is no less important for us than it was for our ancestors in faith. The Eastertime lectionary and sacramentary, seen through our own personal religious experience, are marvelous aids for getting to the heart of the season.

1. How can music evoke the 50-day unity of the Eastertime?

2. How can celebrations of marriage, ordination, confirmation, first communion, anointing of the sick and the dedication of a church during Eastertime enhance our understanding and appreciation of this season?

3. Might it be worthwhile in your parish to organize a special memorial fund for Easter flowers? That way the community can work together to make sure that they are renewed throughout the entire 50 days, forming a visible reminder that the season lasts more than a couple of weeks.

4. What assistance can you give to those who are assigned to preach during the 50 days, so that their message truly bridges the scriptures and human experience?

The death of Jesus was not the end of his power and presence, for he was raised up by the power of God. Nor did it mark the end of the disciples' union with him. After Jesus had appeared to them and when they received the gift of the Spirit, they became apostles of the good news to the ends of the earth. In the face of poverty and persecution they transformed human lives and formed communities which became signs of the power and presence of God. Sharing in the same resurrection faith, contemporary followers of Christ can face the struggles and challenges that await those who bring the gospel vision to bear on our complex economic and social world.

Economic Justice for All, 47

The Fifty Days taken as a unit comprise but a single holy day or feast, at which God gathers his scattered people to himself. He does so by joining them to Christ in the power of the Spirit. For this reason the feast is no longer a mere institution. It has become a person, the person of Christ. Crucified yet risen, he himself is our Pasch. To be gathered together in holy festivity, therefore, is to be gathered into him whose very person is itself the feast now brought to eschatological perfection.

Abbot Patrick Regan

Festivals and Ordinary Time

he seasons of our year are anticipations of festivals and continuations of festivals. Advent and Christmastime go together, as do Lent and Eastertime. Christmas and Easter are our greatest festivals, carrying with them other great days like Epiphany, Ascension and Pentecost. In considering these festivals or others, we need to be serious about the very idea of festivity, for we live in a society that can label such things as "National Buttermilk Week" as if that means something important in people's lives.

Festivals are not made by just naming days: naming and keeping go together. When we speak of these in relation to true festivity, we are asking a great deal of people. Joseph Pieper writes: "To celebrate a festival means: to live out, for some special occasion and in an uncommon manner, the universal assent to the world as a whole" (*In Tune with the World,* page 23). Festivals are without worldly purpose, they are just thanksgiving and praise: "The happiness of being created, the existential goodness of things, the participation in the life of God, the overcoming of death — all these occasions of the great traditional festivals are pure gift" (Pieper, page 46).

Perhaps people of other ages were more ready to acknowledge such pure gift. Certainly it seems to be enough for us to be ready to take Christmas and Easter (and what surrounds them) this way, to let them take us, rather, and bestow on us their gifts. For now, the calendar of the church recognizes that the year should not be filled with lesser festivals that go unrecognized. Instead, we have the steady counting of Ordinary Time between Epiphany and Lent and again from Pentecost until Advent. This offers us a chance to observe fully our original festival, Sunday, kept in the home and in the church community.

The tradition marks certain days throughout the year, mostly during Ordinary Time, to remember and celebrate some of the saints or a mystery of the faith or a title of Mary or Jesus. Only a few of these are likely to carry significance in any particular community, but these few should be identified and kept in special ways. The holy days of obligation are, in each country, an attempt to identify such occasions. Our keeping of Assumption, Immaculate Conception and Mary, Mother of God (the latter two in Advent and Christmastime) celebrate the place of Mary within a parish church. We discuss our observance of the feast of All Saints below. Ascension has its place in the season of Eastertime and Christmas is the center of Advent/Christmastime.

Ordinary Time is marked by the reading of the scriptures in the three-year cycle: Matthew's gospel in Year A, Mark's in B, Luke's in C. The different approaches of these gospels to the life of the church set the tone for the Sunday liturgies and give continuity to each year. The Sundays of Ordinary Time do not call for great productions, but rather for good arrangements of the elements of each liturgy and good use of the gifts of all the various ministers. It is the very ordinariness of these weeks that sustains us and allows the seasons to be so special when they come.

The last weeks of Ordinary Time, the weeks of November, have a special character. On these Sundays we approach the conclusion of the year's gospel and so hear passages that speak of the last things. At the same time, because November comes between the rejoicing of the harvest and the short, dark days of winter, it is a time when people in this climate inevitably focus on death and on the dead. Halloween, with its ghosts and masks and tricks, is a descendant of the spirit of this time. So is the feast of All Saints and November's emphasis on prayer for the dead. Our American Thanksgiving Day also fits into the spirit of this month.

Certainly November is not a season in the same sense as Advent or Lent, but it is a time that seeks to express a certain spirit: the solidarity we profess with the saints and ancestors, something that has a multitude of forms in paintings, windows, statues, relics, cemeteries, litanies, hymns and chants. And all of this is handed on and helps us grow — not only in faith in communion with our saints, but in readiness to acknowledge, with Saint Francis, that in some ways death is a sister to us, another of God's servants.

1. How does the Christian proclamation of the communion of saints express itself in your parish?

2. How does your parish recognize and honor Mary? There are more feasts of Mary in September than in May or any other month; how does your parish observe these?

3. What feasts of the saints are celebrated in your community, in your part of the country? What are some possible directions for these observances?

4. How does your parish observe its patronal feast?

5. What are the liturgies and prayers and devotions of November in your parish?

There are about 32 weeks outside the five church seasons. These weeks are called "Ordinary Time," from the word "ordinal," meaning "counted." Each week is given a number to help us divide the scriptures into readings and to place these in an orderly book called the lectionary. We do the same thing with the church's prayers at Mass, ordered day by day in a book called the Sacramentary.

Ordinary Time is a name for the weeks that come between the church seasons. The period of Ordinary Time that lasts from Eastertime until Advent spans over half the year. In the Northern Hemisphere, most of summer and autumn fall during these weeks. This is harvest time. In the gospels, Jesus often talked about the harvest as a symbol of what heaven might be like. Slowly but surely, as God's creatures grow ripe and then die, they will be harvested into heaven.

Mary Ellen Hynes

The Rites of the Church

The eucharist is and remains the "source and summit" of our encounter with God in Christ. Yet the other rich and various rites of the church provide the foundation, context and entry point that help us all appreciate the centrality of the eucharist in our communal experience of the paschal mystery.

Liturgy brings the individual and the Christian community together before the Lord in the rites of initiation and beginning. It renews them each week in that bond and that presence, and it expresses what happens when two people get married, when we are reconciled to one another, to the church, to God, when we are sick and when we die. In very simple ways the liturgy marks the mornings, the meals and the nights of our lives.

The Liturgy of the Hours

ot many people are thoroughly familiar with this form of communal prayer. Why then does it belong in these notes about the familiar prayers of Catholics?

Long ago, our ancestors in faith had ways for individuals and households to praise and thank God constantly, with the poetic richness of praying at morning and evening with hymns and psalms known by heart. As time went on we lost those forms of prayer. In more recent times, some substitutes were found: the prayers called the morning offering, the act of contrition, the Angelus and other prayers related to the time of day. For some, these too have been lost, and apparently nothing has come to take their place.

Something similar has happened with rituals apart from the Mass. Many popular devotions—devotions to the Sacred Heart or the Sorrowful Mother, and so on—developed during the centuries when the liturgy of the Mass was not something in which most Catholics fully participated. These devotions were usually in the language of the people, with popular hymns, movement, gesture and objects, such as incense and images. These devotions were often very well attended, but in recent years participation in such devotions has dwindled.

It was in these non-eucharistic prayers and devotions that Catholics learned to pray, as individuals, in the family and in small communities. Most Catholics today know only the eucharist as a regular form of communal prayer. Hardly any other shared forms of prayer exist for most parishioners. Without habits and rituals to provide day-in, day-out prayers, to train us in how to pray, to lead us in the ways of praise, petition, thanks and contrition, we have no way to prepare to pray the eucharist, no way to learn how to pray in large gatherings of the church, no way to let the eucharist echo through our week.

We learn to pray by praying, and we learn to pray the Mass through the many ways that ritual prayer enters our lives throughout the day and week. Discovering forms and rhythms of prayer that will resonate with people today has a high priority.

To suggest that the Liturgy of the Hours may be the answer need not bring visions of popularizing the bulky breviary that is usually associated with the clerical form of this prayer. That book is, in fact, the product of a history that began with the simple prayer of all Christians. In the monasteries, this became a very complex pattern of prayer and was lost to the people. Today some are searching for the roots of the Liturgy of the Hours, the best of its earliest forms, in hopes that a truly popular form of morning and evening prayer may again become the daily or weekly prayer of parishes and individuals.

In the simplest form, the praising and thanking of God each morning and evening need not be written down. It is a prayer of memory, known by heart. The basic prayers of this form of prayer are the Lord's Prayer, intercessions and psalms. They can bear repetition, can carry the weight of being used every day in a way that most texts simply cannot. For an individual, the prayer of morning or evening might be one or two short psalms, perhaps with short acclamations and some time for reflection. When several pray together in the parish or at home, simple hymns could be added, along with prayers of intercession. On Sunday afternoons and on some weekday mornings or evenings during Lent, or on festival days, a parish could celebrate a slightly more elaborate Liturgy of the Hours. In any of these settings, the reading of the scriptures might have a place.

The daily living of the faith needs to be strengthened with simple prayer that we might name rites of prayer, in that they are regular and somewhat fixed. These can be in the heart upon rising and preparing for the day, upon coming to table together, and upon retiring at night. In a more elaborate way, they can be the gathered church's prayer between one Sunday eucharist and the next. They need not be created from nothing: We have them; we have always had them, as Jesus himself knew them, in the psalms and the reading of our scripture. Our task is to rediscover the value of the treasure which is already ours.

1. In the Liturgy of the Hours the church—and we are the church!—sanctifies the day. We need to see the rising of the sun and its setting as signs of God caring for creation. Our hope is that the Liturgy of the Hours becomes a satisfying human ritual marking the passage of night and day in our lives.

2. The *General Instruction on the Liturgy of the Hours* provides an outline of the church's theology of prayer. It should be studied carefully as an introduction to the spirituality of daily prayer.

3. How do the Angelus, morning prayers or the sign of the cross at night fulfill the work of this kind of prayer?

4. Has your parish considered the distribution of simple brochures containing a psalm, an acclamation and the Lord's Prayer to every parishioner? A note encouraging them to use it to re-dedicate their days and also as a way of being joined to one another throughout the week might be included with it.

5. What might be some occasions in your parish when the Liturgy of the Hours would be more appropriate than the Mass?

6. What kind of catechesis could your parish offer on the psalms as prayers for today?

Those who plead for the primacy of the prayer of expression over the prayer of empathy ought to remember that the ability to express what is hidden in the heart is a rare gift, and cannot be counted upon by all. What, as a rule, makes it possible for us to pray is our ability to affiliate our own minds with he pattern of fixed texts, to unlock our hearts to the words, and to surrender to their meanings. The words stand before us as living entities full of spiritual power, of a power which often surpasses the grasp of our minds. The words are often the givers, and we the recipients. They inspire our minds and awaken our hearts.

Abraham Joshua Heschel

About the Ignatian method of meditation: it sounds fine to me but I can't do it. I am no good at meditating. This doesn't mean that I get right on with contemplating. I don't do either. If I attempt to keep my mind on the mysteries of the rosary, I am soon thinking about something else, entirely non-religious in nature. So I read my prayers out of the book, prime in the morning and compline at night.

Flannery O'Connor

Christian Initiation of Adults

very society that wants to continue must admit new members. This is true of bowling leagues, universities, the Teamsters, the United States and churches. In some societies, very little may be required to gain admittance: When you wish to become a member of a book or record club, you just send in the coupon and the check. At another extreme, young men gained admission to adulthood in certain African cultures by elaborate rites, as the book and television drama *Roots* depicted. The seriousness surrounding the admission of new members, the length of time involved, the amount of discussion and work between the one asking admission and the group itself—these are some of the signs by which we can evaluate how vital and important the group is to its members.

Moreover, the customs that make up the initiation usually tell the candidate a great deal about the group and the group a great deal about the candidate. It is not unlike the time of engagement before marriage: If these two are to spend their lives together, it is worth the trouble of an initiation time. The rites that have developed and have been used over and over again for the initiation of new members are those that have been proven to work by experience. They let candidate and church make good decisions about one another.

The Catholic church has been rediscovering its rites for the Christian initiation of adults. The patterns in these rites are based on those that were developed in the early centuries of the church when many adults sought admission to the Christian communities. Dioceses and national assemblies of bishops are moving slowly because there is so much at stake. It takes some time to move from the recent tradition of "convert classes" and private instruction before baptism to the full and rich process of the Rite of Christian Initiation of Adults.

The Rite presumes a period of initiation lasting at least a year, and perhaps longer. In the first stage, the person hears the preaching of the gospel. This is a time of inquiry, not to be rushed. The second stage is called the catechumenate. It begins when the candidate formally enters the "order of the catechumens," which, like the "order of the baptized," is a way of belonging in the church. During this time, which may last several months or several years, formation is brought about through contact with the church community and especially with catechists. Catechumens may participate in the liturgy of the word, and the community's keeping of the Christian year is the great teacher of its ways of living and of believing. When both community and catechumen judge that the time is right, the "rite of election" takes place, meaning that the catechumens are now "the elect," the chosen. This happens at the start of Lent. Lent serves as a period of purification and is marked by special rites of "scrutiny" at the Sunday Masses. The church prays that the candidates will be free of all evil. Then, after the Paschal fast of Good Friday and Holy Saturday, the elect profess their faith at the Easter Vigil, are baptized and confirmed, and share for the first time in the eucharist. During the 50 days of Eastertime, the newly baptized continue to come together so that the church may show them the fullness of its life.

In the liturgy, the church puts its life together; thus at liturgy the church expresses itself to the candidates—from their enrollment in the catechumenate until the end of their first Eastertime as Christians. In coming years, these rites will more and more embody ways for the local church to be aware of its catechumens, to be stirred by their presence. But liturgy has to express what is real in people's lives. So the rites of initiation gather up what is really going on: the candidates learning of Christ from those who make up the church, and the church members themselves learning Christ anew from the candidates.

The initiation of adults is much more than just a sacramental ritual bath. If we reduce adult initiation to the rites at the font, we rob the new member of the much-needed love and support and Christian witness that only a flesh-and-blood community can give. The whole process of becoming a Christian, as outlined in the *Rite of Christian Initiation of Adults,* requires the community's involvement in the candidates' journey to baptism. The community passes on the living tradition of faith in ways that no one person or catechism could ever do. Behind all the rites and catechetical preparation, there is a strong sense of welcome. The community opens its arms and warmly receives new members and so integrates them into the community.

1. Study the introduction to the *Rite of Christian Initiation of Adults* and the *National Statutes for the Catechumenate*. How does it compare with current parish practices of receiving adults into the church?

2. What is the wisdom in the requirement in *Statute* 6 that catechumens experience a full liturgical year?

3. Seek out some people who have recently joined the church. What do they have to say about their initiation that could help future parish plans?

4. How can the parish minister to adults after baptism? What is your parish doing about faith-sharing and small Christian communities among those already baptized?

Here is born in Spirit-soaked fertility

a brood destined for another City,

begotten by God's blowing

and borne upon this torrent

by the Church their virgin mother.

Reborn in these depths they reach for heaven's realm,

the born-but-once unknown by felicity.

The spring is life that floods the world,

the wounds of Christ its awesome source.

Sinner sink beneath the sacred surf

that swallows age and spits up youth.

Sinner here scour sin away down to innocence,

for they know no enmity who are by

one font, one Spirit, one faith made one.

Sinner shudder not a sin's kind and number,

for those born here are holy.

Inscription in the baptistry

of St. John Lateran,

the cathedral church of Rome;

translated by Aidan Kavanagh

Infant Baptism

baby makes a difference. Parents know that, and older brothers and sisters know it too. Things change. They have to. Adjustments are made, and the long process of taking this person from total helplessness to something like maturity begins. Society, in the person of the neighbors and relations, medical personnel and even the business world, prepares parents for their new lives before the birth of the baby. Baby showers help provide necessary equipment as well as advice. Questions and answers about sex, weight and name get everyone through the first days. The larger society also takes notice: making future room in schools, work places, shopping centers.

The church also observes the birth of a baby in its community. The baptism of infants is the most visible manifestation of this notice. This rite, revised after Vatican II to acknowledge the reality that this is an infant and not just a small adult being baptized, is a gathering of the church around the couple and their child. Just as with adults, the initiation is initiation into a community, but here it is the community's part to pledge itself to be a source of nourishment, of faith, of a gospel-filled way of life.

Parishes often ask parents to attend preparation sessions before the child is born. These gatherings provide opportunities for the parents to meet the parish staff and parishioners who have taken on this special ministry. Here they can discuss the commitment they make in having their child baptized, and find out something about how the parish can support them in this commitment. In a process like this, the parents can make a decision about the baptism, and the pastor can see that they are serious in their intention to make a home where their child can learn trust and love and faith from the very first. Then the baptism is planned.

In the child's baptism, parents and community express commitment. That is why the community needs to be present: Its support is real, not theoretical. In practice, that commitment might be shown by the presence of a special minister who works with the families before, during and after the baptism. These ministers would be people who have gifts for getting to know people quickly and putting them at ease. They want to show the parents a church whose concern is to help with their real needs and not just to impose its own patterns on them. These ministers see to it that the church does not forget about the child during the years between baptism and first communion. They know how important these first years are to all that comes after, and how much support parents need at this time.

The rite of infant baptism itself should be scheduled so that it can be a festive welcoming of the child and a strong affirmation of the faith and commitment of the parents and the community.

The celebration may take place at Sunday Mass, since the presence of the community is so important, but baptisms at Sunday Mass should not be scheduled too often. Appropriate days would include Easter above all others, the Baptism of the Lord and perhaps the patronal feast of the parish. Within the rite, the acclamations of the assembly, voicing their support for the parents and rejoicing at the baptism itself, need to be strong, with song or applause or other clear signs. Recent documents make clear the church's preference for baptism by immersion, so that the symbol of the water, spoken of so well in its blessing, may be clear to everyone present. The baptismal garment and candle are to be beautiful objects, witnessing what has happened.

When an infant is baptized, our attention very naturally is on him or her. But the parents deserve attention too, for they are the ones who at this baptism commit themselves to raising their child in faith. They need support and encouragement, prayer and good example to fulfill their vocation as Christian parents. They may be newcomers to the neighborhood or infrequent worshipers. Even for active and practicing parents, the baptism of a child can be an occasion of further initiation into the church's life.

1. How does the parish family show its support to parents at the time of baptism?

2. What happens to a child between baptism and the first year of school? What things are learned, and what directions are set? At baptism, parents promise a Christian home and the community promises to support the parents in this. How can the community show this support during the first five years of the child's life?

3. Does the parish library provide books that parents can use in enlivening the stories of faith for their little children?

Snatching her baby free, she thrust it at me

almost roughly, the gesture saying "Take it!"

And I did. Clasping the baby to me.

Then she snatched away her baby;

and another woman was thrusting her baby.

Then another, and another . . . Until I had

embraced probably a dozen babies.

I wouldn't learn until maybe a year later,

from a Harvard University professor,

Dr. Jerome Bruner, a scholar of such matters,

"You didn't know you were participating in one

of the oldest ceremonies of humankind,

called the laying on of hands. In their way,

they were telling you 'through this flesh,

which is us, we are you, and you are us!'"

Alex Haley

Confirmation

he debate within the church about this sacrament is reflected in the variety of ages suggested for its celebration. In some places, the church confirms infants when they are baptized. In other areas, confirmation may come at the same time as first communion. The practice in much of this country has been to confirm during the junior high years, but a few places have moved in the direction of a much later time, letting confirmation come as the mark of a more mature decision for membership in the church. There is general agreement that confirmation is historically a sacrament of initiation, along with baptism and eucharist, but there is disagreement about its use in the church today.

In most places, for now, the celebrations of this sacrament are for large groups of young people. It is important that the liturgy is a strong expression of the church's life in the Spirit, a strong expression of the church's prayer that the Spirit be strong in those confirmed. An exclusive emphasis on maturity in a sort of updated "soldiers of Christ" theology is inadequate.

In the liturgy, the presence of the candidates is primary. In fact, their presence should be clear to the whole parish in the weeks before the confirmation: by praying for them publicly, by the presence of the group with their sponsors at Sunday Masses. At the confirmation liturgy, their individual names need to be heard, and each face seen. They are not a "confirmation class," a crowd of anonymous seventh or eighth graders: They are so many individuals, each one of whom has requested confirmation and has been found ready, each one of whom has a sponsor and the pastor to testify to that readiness. The candidates and sponsors should help in the preparation of the confirmation liturgy, learning about and especially experiencing the power and the history of the laying on of hands and the anointing with perfumed oil.

Confirmation ordinarily means the presence of the bishop. Plans for the liturgy should allow him, as presider, to relate directly to the candidates and to the whole assembly.

If the liturgy is concelebrated, this should not obscure the relationship among the bishop, the candidates and the rest of the assembly. Within the liturgy, the bishop might be introduced and welcomed. Since he is probably not familiar with the local practices in the liturgy, all the other ministers should be very well rehearsed in their roles and have a feeling for the overall flow of the liturgy. This can free the bishop to preside, to be completely present to the candidates and to the assembly.

The liturgy should be simple, without additional elements that are intended to give solemnity but, in fact, obscure or weaken the central symbols of laying on of hands, anointing and eucharist. Preparation rites can set a festive mood. The liturgy of the word proceeds much as on any Sunday.

In the rite of confirmation, after the gospel, the candidates are called by name to come forward; the bishop addresses the candidates in the homily. The rites that follow should proceed without commentary or explanation. Everything should be arranged so that the imposition of hands, with the silence that comes before, is a most powerful experience. That can happen when all attention is on the bishop and the candidates, when the silence is total, when the gesture is full and the prayer is well spoken or sung, when the "Amen" is like the great Amen at the conclusion of the eucharistic prayer. Then all should be able to see the chrism, the oil mixed with fragrant perfume and blessed by the bishop on Holy Thursday. The anointing is to make generous use of the oil, and the oil is not to be wiped off afterward; if anything, it should be rubbed in. The fragrance of the chrism should fill the whole room. The vessel used for the oil, its rich fragrance, even carrying the oil in the entrance procession and honoring it with incense: All help to transform the anointing from a mysterious bit of tradition to a beautiful rite of the church, honoring and strengthening the presence of the Holy Spirit in its members.

After the anointing, the table is prepared for the eucharist, which should be a festive banquet.

1. In the Eastern Rites of the Catholic church this rite is called chrismation, because the chrism itself, the core symbol, bespeaks God's action, sealing in the gift of the Spirit. What can be done to heighten the candidates' appreciation of this blessed oil?

2. How do we deepen our appreciation of the deep connection between baptism and confirmation?

3. How can we avoid making confirmation look like a class exercise?

4. How can confirmation become a parish-wide celebration?

The sign of Christ is traced on the part of the body that is most immediately visible to anyone who meets us. Nothing is more difficult for us to hide than that which is in any way written on our forehead. Anyone who has ever had to wear even a small band-aid on the forehead after a mishap can attest to the truth of what I am saying.

Chrism is produced by adding aromatic essences (especially balsam) to olive oil. Here again the element of public manifestation that is proper to confirmation exercises its influence. Paul says of Christians that they should be "the aroma of Christ" (2 Corinthians 2:14). Wherever Christians live their baptism and confirmation in an authentic way, they emit as it were a "strong and wholesome fragrance."

How can anyone observe Mother Teresa at work serving the starving children of Calcutta and not smell something of this strong and wholesome fragrance, this aroma of Christ? This woman has translated into action what the bishop meant when on the day of her confirmation he laid his hand on her head and anointed her forehead so that she might confess her faith and bear witness to it.

Balthasar Fisher

Weddings

hen two people marry, the whole complex gathering of rites—some from the state, some from the family, some from the church—serves many purposes. For one, they show what all these groups think about marriage, and they try to impress these understandings on the couple. For another, they let everyone adjust to the idea that there is something new among us: We cannot think of these two tomorrow as we thought of them yesterday. And yet another task of the rites: Some of them are meant to allow us to express our sheer delight in the festival. When ritual does its work, all these things happen. But there are sometimes difficulties when it comes to the church's part in the wedding. If the couple has no feeling of belonging, they are likely to be indifferent, seeing what happens in the church building as only another obligation. Apart from the bridal party's entrance procession and a favorite song or two, they may say that "anything Father wants is fine with us."

Our goal is for people to feel they belong in the church and know that the church's ritual is their own expression of what marriage means. It is often possible to begin with a sense that this wedding is a gathering of the church, the plain old small-c church: friends and relatives with all their faults and even lack of faith. It is these people, with their hopes and tears and sighs, who are the gathered church. It is their faith and their love, kindled by the marrying couple and encouraged by the presider's leadership, that celebrates the sacrament. It is a family, a community of friends, a church, that celebrates. An understanding like this will enrich the couple's experience, and prevent their approaching their wedding as a predetermined formula indifferent to them or as a stage for them to celebrate themselves.

Something has to happen between the church gathered here and the couple, something beyond the legal and social, something bound up with being the church. When we find or lose a job, when we move from one place to another, when a child grows up and moves away—these are crucial moments, times for prayer, but they are not times when we call the church together. A wedding is something more: more profound, more lasting. Our hope and our faith and our support need to be expressed in the church's ritual in ways that are simply not possible in the other social and legal rites of the wedding. In the liturgy of the wedding, we seek the deepest signs of what this church here, and the whole church, believes: gratitude to God for bringing this about, trust in God's strength and grace to see it through, intercession for the couple and for all the church and world.

The ritual is to make such things felt, seen, heard and touched. With songs, processions, greetings, prayers, scriptures and silent reflection, the assembled friends and family join in the ritual with the couple. Such a spirit brings about the right moment for the couple to answer the questions put to them and to answer about freedom, about fidelity, about a Christian home and family. And it brings about the right moment for the vows, a profound moment, with clear, firm words spoken by and to each partner so that all can hear and can respond with some sign of affirmation. The giving and receiving of the rings expresses in one of our most ancient symbols the union and the hope that it lasts forever. The blessing of the marriage, which comes some time later if the eucharist is celebrated, is a chance for all present to voice all that is in their hearts for the future good of these two.

This involves more than choosing among the alternatives for scripture selections or picking out good songs. There is the presumption that the rite itself is celebrated well, with a presider and other ministers who do their tasks well, with a flow to the ritual that creates community among the guests and lets them express what is in their hearts, with a place for the couple to make their vows before the Lord and the church.

1. Discussion about a wedding liturgy can begin and end with the selection of music and scriptures. These are important, but there is much more to be considered. There is the gathering time and the procession, the roles of the bride and groom as ministers of the sacrament, the role of the assembly and the inclusion of particular ethnic rituals. How does your parish help plan these elements for weddings?

2. Why do you think so many engaged couples are willing to settle for "whatever Father wants"?

3. How can a congregation give expression to its joy and gratitude at the wedding liturgy?

4. When the assembly is brought into the celebration, their participation is a real support to the marrying couple in living out their commitment. Yet the assembly's role is often ignored. It often appears that they have gathered to watch the action or photograph it rather than participate in it. But the celebration of Christian marriage is really a community celebration. The whole church is blessed in this couple. There is a great joy in the witnessing the community does. How do the ministers urge and invite the full, active and conscious participation of the assembly at every wedding liturgy?

5. Many parishes provide an assortment of articles and other helpful ideas for the couple as they prepare the liturgy of marriage. What resources do you make available in your parish to help couples prepare their wedding liturgy?

Many times a day Abraham would take Ann in his arms and hug her and kiss her and tell her he loved her. If he left the house for even a few minutes he would kiss her and tell her he loved her. He didn't need to tell her. She knew that he loved her. But the telling was a pleasure. And every day, also, he told her she was beautiful, and when he did she would go and sit in his lap and he would kiss her and tell her he loved her, and she told him she loved him again and again, for her love for him was always welling up and overflowing, and it was a pleasure to be able always to tell him, without embarrassment, how she loved him, without restraint, she loved him, without fear that her love wouldn't be returned. It was returned, over and over, and she never got tired of hearing it.

Sherril Jaffe

The quality of our commitments reveals the values we live by and determines the meaningfulness of the tasks we perform. In each phase of our lives, new questions about our old commitments arise. Does our continued attendance at Sunday worship, for example, indicate a deeper commitment to Gospel values or only the security of familiar rituals? Does a wedding anniversary celebrate past or renewed commitments to another person?

Regis Duffy

Reconciliation

n the family, the school, the workplace — in any community — there must be attention to healing. People hurt each other, let the hurt done to them grow into a greater hurt done to someone else. Choices are made based on something other than the greatest good of all. However such things show themselves, we know in small and great ways the presence of evil — not just out there but inside. And we try, when we can, to find ways to bring healing.

The church, every church, every gathering that professes to live by the words of the scriptures and to find itself in the breaking of bread, knows that all this hurting and all this healing is at the heart of what being church is about: that God is greater than evil, that God loves us despite the evil that we do, that there is reconciliation. Every gathering of the church proclaims this. Such direction toward reconciliation, not just as an insight of theology but as a reality in our communities, is especially celebrated in the eucharist. In the one loaf and one cup, in the praying of the Our Father, in the greeting of peace, and in the common eating and drinking of the Lord's body and blood, we share a vision of God's kingdom, where all the hurt we do each other ends. But the church is not satisfied with a "pie in the sky when we die" vision: The eating and the drinking in holy communion are lies if they do not reflect a present striving.

The church knows rites other than eucharist that focus on the reconciliation of an individual with the larger community, or that mark our common effort to repent, to struggle against evil. The season of Lent developed not only to support the initiation of new Christians, but also to observe acts of penance and reconciliation by people who had seriously offended the Lord's commandments and the ways of the community. Lent became a time when the whole church sought mightily to turn from evil and walk in the way of the Lord.

While we are discovering the dimensions of reconciliation present in the eucharist and seek what the season of Lent can be for us today, we are also renewing the rites of reconciliation themselves. One direction that seems to reflect the way we experience evil and the greater grace of God leads toward communal penance services. Perhaps these can be associated with Lent or with other recurring days (as the ember days were) so that patterns are established in the parish. The rites themselves, with the reading of scripture and much silence, appropriate music and a gesture of reconciliation, must be planned and carried out well so that they bear the weight of what is being expressed. People are more and more aware that sin is not something that can be separated into small, individual portions. Prejudice, hunger, war-making — these make it clear that evil is contagious and powerful in our world and touches all of us. And we are more accustomed to seeing how our lives move in broad directions, how the ways we share in evil or in good cannot readily be isolated; things interconnect. We strive to let grace more and more be our way.

All of this we want to express in ritual. Sometimes this is best done in the large gathering of the church, and sometimes in a simple meeting of individual penitent and confessor. In the latter case, we need to explore the possibilities of the new rite, which stresses prayer, scripture reading and the laying on of hands, as well as dialogue between penitent and confessor.

Reconciliation, like all church rituals, is more than a ritual: It is the church's way of life. The healing nature of the church needs to be evident in all the parish does. Every sinner must know that he or she is welcome in the community where mercy and compassion await. And the community cannot wait until the alienated seek reconciliation; the community must spread the word that forgiveness and healing are gifts freely given. For any of us to pretend that we have no wounds, or that they will heal by themselves, is an illusion. We need God's healing forgiveness and we need each other to be assured that forgiveness is real.

1. What can help communities develop a sense of the importance of communal reconciliation services?

2. Has your parish ever used the "Rite of Reconciliation of Several Penitents with Individual Confession and Absolution" from the 1974 *Rite of Penance?*

3. How can a life of reconciliation be fostered in a parish? How do we get beyond individualistic morality?

4. Do you know the eucharistic prayers for reconciliation? Are they appropriately used in the parish?

The best way to fulfill one's obligations of justice and love is to contribute to the common good according to one's means and the needs of others, and also to promote and help public and private organizations devoted to bettering the conditions of life. There are people who profess noble sentiments and who in practice, however, are carelessly indifferent to the needs of society. There are many in various countries who make light of social laws and directives and are not ashamed to resort to fraud and cheating to avoid paying just taxes and fulfilling other social obligations. There are others who neglect the norms of social conduct, such as those regulating public hygiene and speed limits, forgetting that they are endangering their own lives and the lives of others by their carelessness.

All must consider it their sacred duty to count social obligations among their chief duties today and observe them as such. For the more closely the world comes together, the more widely do people's obligations transcend particular groups and extend to the whole world. This will be realized only if individuals and groups practice moral and social virtues and foster them in social living. Then, under the necessary help of divine grace, there will arise a generation of new women and men, the molders of a new humanity.

**The Pastoral Constitution
on the Church in the Modern World,** *30*

Anointing of the Sick

roups of people who have organized to educate, to play ball, or even just to make money take notice when one of the group is hurt or sick. We have ways of responding to this: sending cards, sending flowers, telephoning, going to visit. The words we use in such situations follow familiar patterns as we offer good wishes, reassurances, jokes. We seem to know that there is healing in our presence, in person or in a gift, and in familiar words.

As the church, we know from the prophets and from Jesus about the importance of visiting and caring for the sick. This, in an organized way, has been one of the great works of the church: hospitals founded and staffed by religious sisters. Concern for the sick and for all who cannot defend themselves causes the church, in its very best moments, to raise its voice against any kind of oppression.

From the first, continuing Jesus' care for the sick, the church has gathered to pray for those who suffer. To show this concern, to allow the assembled church (whether few or many) to bring the sick person before the Lord, there is the laying on of hands. This brings a sense of solidarity with the one who is sick and with those who are healthy. This is perhaps our richest symbol, this simple touching in silence. To those who are sick, the laying on of hands makes clear what is really true: They are never alone, never cut off from the community. But the gesture must be true, must not be alone, must not be apart from the community. The church must be telling the truth when it lays on hands. This is not "administering a sacrament," but rather letting the sacrament embody what happens between the community and one who is sick. The title of the rite of anointing makes this clear: *Pastoral Care of the Sick*.

The anointing itself is not the only time of prayer with those who are sick. The parish helps those who have a special ministry to the sick to learn how to be with and pray with the sick. The rite makes this clear simply by the fact that the ritual of anointing is part of a collection of rites called *Pastoral Care of the Sick: Rites of Anointing and Viaticum*. Here we see that the anointing is just one time of prayer with those who are sick. The parish's ministers of care also visit the sick, pray with them, bring them holy communion. Clergy, deacons and ministers of care need a firm grasp of the approach and the particulars of these rites for the sick and dying, which were published in 1983.

The people of a church need to know that this sacrament, and the other times of prayer that surround it, may be celebrated when there is serious illness of any kind, and that the very young as well as the elderly may need the prayer of the church. Learning about the sacrament may come about through the good practice of communal celebrations, where many sick and elderly persons gather with other members of the church. In a nursing home or in the parish church, the community gathers to pray with and for the sick and elderly. Such occasions need careful planning (not only of the liturgy but of transportation and other details), but can become a worthy and regular expression of the life of this church.

One way the community can express its concern for members who are ill is to plan a communal celebration of the sacrament of anointing of the sick within the celebration of the eucharist. Here, in the parish church, the anointed can experience in a profound way the loving care of the Christian family. This involves more than just scheduling. Well before the liturgy there has to be personal contact with those who will be anointed. Arrangements must be made for transportation. This is a good occasion to call people to service in the ministry of healing.

1. Consider the power of touch. What has it meant to you in illness, or when you helped to heal with your power of touch?

2. How might a communal celebration of the anointing of the sick affect the community's understanding of the sacrament?

3. Is there an appropriate day or time of year that is particularly suitable for an annual liturgy of the anointing of the sick?

4. What catechesis needs to happen so that people understand the liturgy as one of healing and strengthening, not reserved for those at death's door?

I have never been anywhere but sick. In a sense sickness is a place, more instructive than a long trip to Europe, and it's always a place where there's no company, where nobody can follow. Sickness before death is a very appropriate thing and I think those who don't have it miss one of God's mercies.

Flannery O'Connor

❖

"Poor soul!" murmured Mandy. She put Grandma's feet in the tub and, crouching beside it, slowly, slowly rubbed her swollen legs. Mandy was tired, too. Mrs. Harris sat in her nightcap and shawl, her hands crossed in her lap. She never asked for this greatest solace of the day; it was something that Mandy gave, who had nothing else to give. If there could be a comparison in absolutes, Mandy was the needier of the two — but she was younger. The kitchen was quiet and full of shadow, with only the light from and old lantern. Neither spoke. Mrs. Harris dozed from comfort, and Mandy herself was half asleep as she performed one of the oldest rites of compassion.

Willa Cather

Funerals

s at birth and marriage, so at death: The rites of a community serve several purposes. They convey a great deal about how death is understood in the group, and about what relationship there is between the living and dead. They may also convey something of the meaning of this individual's life. The rites will handle the time of transition from life with this person present in the community to life with this person absent. This recognizes that death ordinarily brings a group — family, neighborhood, church — into a different way of being. Changes like this are always difficult. They may challenge the existence of the group itself, or at the least call people to new roles and new understandings.

Rites, however, are not and cannot be rational attempts to do all these things. They are the ways people do these things for themselves, and they work at levels far deeper than the rational.

The rites that surround death manifest very clearly a problem in our culture. The usual practices of mortuaries and cemeteries carry certain messages about the meaning of death, about this individual, about how grief is handled. Seldom do these have any relation to the convictions expressed in the rituals of the church. As with weddings, the church's ritual is often the loser: It is treated as one of the things that Father does, or as a support for the message of the funeral director. Parishes concerned with the ways that the church's ritual can be a strong and worthy expression of our faith study the rites and the many options available in the *Order of Christian Funerals,* form a ministry of those who can help grieving families to make the rites their own, seek to educate funeral and cemetery directors to the church's best practice, and use the month of November each year to ponder death and the communion of saints.

In particular, the parish ministers to the dying and to mourners. The church's prayer with the dying is not "extreme unction," which is now understood and practiced as the anointing of the sick, but viaticum, final communion. There are many beautiful prayers in our tradition that praise God for the love that God has shown to this person in life, and express deep confidence in the communion of saints, the community that transcends death. These prayers continue through the hour of death and may end with the blessing of the body. In some cases, a priest or deacon is present, but we should know these as the prayers of family and friends. Consult the book of *Catholic Household Blessings and Prayers,* especially pages 267–280 and 335–350.

The wake service is a combination of structured and unstructured moments. The ritual should be in continuity with the less formal moments of gathering and greeting, sharing stories and memories, offering sympathy. The wake is often more intimate than the funeral, and it is more clearly centered on the one who has died. The wake can be a good beginning for the long process of coming to terms with life now that this person is gone. The community shows its support in the wake, the support that will be there in the weeks and months to come.

The funeral liturgy, which usually includes the celebration of the eucharist, allows for scripture readings and liturgical music and various other elements to be chosen by the family or other mourners. In this liturgy and in the rites that take place at the side of the grave, the church holds parting and communion in tension: There is the final commendation of the deceased to the Lord, and the reality of the grave itself, as we console ourselves in faith in our communion with the saints and our waiting for the resurrection of the dead and the life of the world to come. The rites take these things and give them powerful expression in song, word and gesture.

1. The family of one who has died, and all the friends that make up a community, want a good funeral. What goes into such a funeral? Have you participated in some? What would make your own funeral good?

2. Our rites are not attempts to hide grief. Our Christian liturgy does not deny loss and emptiness. At the wake, family and friends are helped to face death. They need the opportunity to share aloud memories of the one who has died. The story of the dead Christian needs to be told: Family and friends must not leave all the words to the clergy, who may not have known the deceased very well. The *Order of Christian Funerals* suggests that at the final commendation in the church, the family may speak to those assembled. This does not mean the funeral becomes a long eulogy; it means that there is a place for personal expression.

   Family and friends are not subjected to the funeral ritual, but are brought into the rites and prayers, making the liturgy of the church a real aid to the bereaved in burying their dead.

   How might the family be helped to participate more in the funeral rites at the wake? At the church? At the cemetery?

3. Apart from the funeral rites, how can a parish foster a good spirituality of death? Think about things your parish can do to broaden its bereavement ministry.

The Church through its funeral rites commends the dead to God's merciful love and pleads for the forgiveness of their sins. At the funeral rites, especially at the celebration of the eucharistic sacrifice, the Christian community affirms and expresses the union of the Church on earth with the Church in heaven in the one great communion of saints. Though separated from the living, the dead are still at one with the community of believers on earth and benefit from their prayers and intercession. At the rite of final commendation and farewell, the community acknowledges the reality of separation and commends the deceased to God. In this way it recognizes the spiritual bond that still exists between the living and the dead and proclaims its belief that all the faithful will be raised up and reunited in the new heavens and a new earth, where death will be no more.

General Introduction

to the Order of Christian Funerals, 6

In Conclusion

ver twenty years ago, in 1973, the Vatican's Sacred Congregation for Divine Worship issued a document called the *Directory for Masses with Children*. What it has to say goes beyond planning Masses with children. It is important for any consideration of how the church prays.

In the introductory paragraphs, the document makes some statements about the creation of a whole environment, a way of living, in which prayer will be possible and real for children—or for any of us. "Children are prepared for eucharistic communion and introduced more deeply into its meaning. It is not right to separate such liturgical and eucharistic formation from the general human and Christian education of children. Indeed it would be harmful if liturgical formation lacked such a foundation." (8)

The preparation for praying the eucharist is not learning *about* eucharistic liturgy, it is simply learning to pray, to be at home with song and gesture and all that our rituals involve. But this is not something that can exist in a different world, its own box. For example, the holiness of the altar table and of the sharing in the bread and cup is not learned in isolation. A sense of that holiness depends on the child—or anyone—experiencing in the family a sense of the holiness of all food and of the meal taken together. When these experiences are deep and rich, a person can have a feel for what we are about at eucharist. Without that, the liturgy necessarily becomes something apart from what the person is and does.

This puts our prayer in a larger and realistic context. Teaching children to pray, for example, is not a matter of first learning the Lord's Prayer, or having the family together each Sunday at Mass. It is a matter of a way of living: What things are important to the family, how prayer centers them. Song together at table, thanksgiving and intercession at bedtime, time for reading and reflection on the Sunday scriptures, customs and prayers to mark the seasons—these teach prayer when they are important to the parents, part of normal life. Day by day and week by week, these reflect a sense of God's presence that fills all of life.

When people gather for eucharist, the *Directory* tells us, there are some qualities that should be observed: "In this way even if children already have some feeling for God and the things of God, they may also experience the human values which are found in the eucharistic celebration, depending upon their age and personal progress. These values are the activity of the community, exchange of greetings, capacity to listen and to seek and grant pardon, expression of gratitude, experience of symbolic actions, a meal of friendship, and festive celebration" (9). That awesome list describes the human experience. We may or may not be able to verbalize it, but after a parish Sunday Mass, we should have a sense of having been at a meal of friendship, a festive celebration. We should feel that we have really put words and gestures to our thanksgiving to God. The *Directory* wants us to be careful about saying what happens at Mass in theological language, or on some spiritual level, if we have not tended first to the human experience on which all else depends.

And that has been a unifying element through these pages, to discover how much we know and feel about good ritual, yet do not always bring to our liturgy because we have not made the connections, or because we have thought the church's prayer to be only a matter of history and documents and rubrics. No; the church's prayer is much more a matter of real people and their very real spirit.

Resources

Collections

Deiss, Lucian, ed., *Springtime of the Liturgy* (Collegeville: The Liturgical Press, 1979). A collection of texts from and about the liturgy taken from the first centuries of the church.

Documents on the Liturgy, 1963–1979: Conciliar, Papal and Curial Texts (Collegeville: The Liturgical Press, 1982). This 1500-page volume is the finest resource for the documents themselves, with excellent indexes and notes. It contains not only those texts that are concerned entirely with liturgy, but portions of other documents which have implications for liturgy.

Jones, Cheslyn, et al., *The Study of Liturgy,* 2nd ed. (New York: Oxford University Press, 1992). A collection of chapters by various scholars, offering in-depth information on theology, history and pastoral aspects of liturgy. Thorough bibliography included.

Lee, Bernard J. ed., *Alternative Futures for Worship* (seven volumes) (Collegeville: The Liturgical Press, 1987). A series of books looking to the future of the liturgy, covering such topics as theology, initiation, eucharist, reconciliation, Christian marriage, anointing of the sick, ministry and leadership.

Martimort, A. G. ed., *The Church at Prayer* (Collegeville: The Liturgical Press, 1992). Presents a detailed survey of the development of Catholic worship from both historical and theological perspectives.

The Liturgy Documents: A Parish Resource 3rd ed., (Chicago: Liturgy Training Publications, 1991). The most basic documents of the liturgical renewal including the *Constitution on the Sacred Liturgy,* the *General Instruction of the Roman Missal, Norms for the Liturgical Year,* excerpts from the *Ceremonial of Bishops,* the *Directory for Masses with Children, This Holy and Living Sacrifice: Directory for the Celebration and Reception of Communion under Both Kinds;* and, from the United States Bishops' Committee on the Liturgy, *Music in Catholic Worship, Environment and Art in Catholic Worship* and *Fulfilled in your Hearing: The Homily in the Sunday Assembly.* A short commentary on each document by a prominent scholar is provided, as is a complete index.

Sourcebooks from Liturgy Taining Publications: *Advent, Christmas, Lent* (2 volumes), *Triduum* (3 volumes), *Easter, Baptism, Eucharist, Reconciliation, Marriage, Music, Liturgy, Death.* These collections of reflections, sayings and passages from the tradition on the liturgical year and on the sacraments are wonderful resources for prayer, preaching and study.

Prayer Sources

Book of Common Worship (Louisville: Westminster/ John Knox Press, 1993). A resource for all the major rites of the Presbyterian Church. It should be in every liturgy library.

Byzantine Daily Worship (Allendale NJ: Alleluia Press, 1995). This prayer book includes portions of the Office, the Divine Liturgy and prayers from the liturgical year. This is a magnificent part of the Christian tradition, far too little known to most Western Christians.

Lutheran Book of Worship (Minneapolis: Augsburg Publishing House, 1979). With its companion volumes (especially *Book of Occasional Services*), this is a rich resource of prayers, scripture, hymns and rites.

The Book of Blessings (New York: Catholic Book Publishing Company, 1989). This is the official book of blessings of the Catholic Church containing prayers, readings, services and blessings for many occasions.

The Book of Common Prayer, rev. ed. (New York: The Seabury Press, 1979). Together with its companion volume, *The Book of Occasional Services,* (Church Hymnal Corporation, 1979), this prayer book of the Episcopal Church forms a rich source of fine prayer texts for the seasons and sacraments.

Periodicals

Assembly, Notre Dame: Center for Pastoral Liturgy. Five times a year, eight pages. Each issue explores the tradition, meaning and practice of some aspect of the liturgical event in order to help the community and its ministers enter more deeply into the spirit of the liturgy. Contact LTP, 1800 N. Hermitage, Chicago IL 60622; phone

1-800-933-1800; fax 1-800-933-7094; e-mail orders@ltp.org.

Catechumenate, Chicago: Liturgy Training Publications. Bimonthly. A magazine aimed at supporting those involved in the ministry of Christian initiation. Contact LTP, 1800 N. Hermitage, Chicago IL 60622; phone 1-800-933-1800; fax 1-800-933-7094; e-mail orders@ltp.org.

Environment and Art Letter, Chicago: Liturgy Training Publications. Monthly. A newsletter geared toward artists and designers and anyone involved with church building renovation or design. Contact LTP, 1800 N. Hermitage, Chicago IL 60622; phone 1-800-933-1800; fax 1-800-933-7094; e-mail orders@ltp.org.

Liturgical Ministry, Collegeville: The Liturgical Press. Quarterly. Each issue of this journal focuses on one topic with some articles giving a scholarly update and other articles offering a pastoral focus. Contact The Liturgical Press, Saint John's Abbey, PO Box 7500, Collegeville MN 56321-7500.

Liturgy 90, Chicago: Liturgy Training Publications. Eight times a year. Features on the seasons and sacraments, columns on music, environment and art, questions and answers. Newsletter of Chicago's Office for Divine Worship. Contact LTP, 1800 N. Hermitage, Chicago IL 60622; phone 1-800-933-1800; fax 1-800-933-7094; e-mail orders@ltp.org.

Liturgy, Washington: The Liturgical Conference. Quarterly, 88 pages. The journal of the Liturgical Conference, an ecumenical membership organization. Each issue explores a single aspect of liturgy, usually taking in many disciplines and many church traditions. Back issues are available and are an excellent resource. Contact The Liturgical Conference, 806 Rhode Island Avenue NE, Washington DC 20018.

Modern Liturgy, San Jose, California: Liturgy Resources Publications. Published 10 times a year. Articles cover a variety of topics, usually with a pastoral application. Modern Liturgy, 160 E. Virginia Street #290, San Jose CA 95112.

National Bulletin on Liturgy, Ottawa: National Liturgical Office. Six times a year, 64 pages. Each issue explores one topic in detail, often with extensive bibliography. Contact National Liturgical Office, 90 Parent Avenue, Ottawa, Ontario K1N 7B1 CANADA.

Pastoral Music, Washington: National Association of Pastoral Musicians. Six times a year, 48 pages. Often several major articles on a single theme together with many reviews and announcements. Centers on music but touches on all areas of liturgy. Contact NPM, 225 Sheridan Street NW, Washington DC 20011-1492.

Plenty Good Room, Chicago: Liturgy Training Publications. Bimonthly. A magazine that gives support to those who minister with black Catholics and their liturgies. Contact LTP, 1800 N. Hermitage, Chicago IL 60622; phone 1-800-933-1800; fax 1-800-933-7094; e-mail orders@ltp.org.

Worship, Collegeville: The Order of Saint Benedict. Six times a year, 96 pages. This scholarly journal has been a primary support of the liturgical renewal in the English-speaking world since 1926. Contact Saint John's Abbey, Collegeville MN 56321-7500.

Language Issues in Celebrating the Liturgy

Bishops' Committee on the Liturgy, "Criteria for the Evaluation of Inclusive Language," *BCL Newsletter* (October 1990). Official guidelines for proceeding with inclusive language.

Canadian Conference of Catholic Bishops, "Workshops on Inclusive Language," CCCB Publications Service (1990). Methods for proceeding with and educating toward inclusive language.

Huels, John, "Liturgy, Inclusive Language, and Canon Law," in *Living No Longer for Ourselves,* Kathleen Hughes and Mark Francis, eds. (Collegeville: The Liturgical Press, 1991). Various essays showing the role of inclusive language in Catholic liturgy today.

Resources for *First Things*

Bouyer, Louis, *Rite and Man: Natural Sacredness and Christian Liturgy* (Notre Dame: University of Notre Dame Press, 1963). Classic study of the sacredness of our fundamental rituals.

Kavanagh, Aidan, *Elements of Rite* (Collegeville: The Liturgical Press, 1982). A classic statement about liturgy containing some rules, laws, principles and common errors: an honest and often devastating look at Christians and their rituals.

Klauser, Theodor, *A Short History of the Western Liturgy* (New York: Oxford, 1979). A readable survey of the development of the Christian eucharistic liturgy.

Power, David N., *Unsearchable Riches: The Symbolic Nature of Liturgy* (Collegeville: The Liturgical Press, 1992). Power writes to call forth a new appreciation of symbol and also to appreciate the culture's critical stance.

Richter, Klemens, *The Meaning of the Sacramental Symbols* (Collegeville: The Liturgical Press, 1990). A comprehensive examination of the symbols used in worship, including origins and meaning for today.

White, James, *Introduction to Christian Worship,* rev. ed. (Nashville: Abingdon, 1990). Ecumenically based overview of the principles and practices of Christian worship.

Resources for *The Elements of Liturgy*

Buscemi, John, *Meeting House Essays: Places for Devotion* (Chicago: Liturgy Training Publications, 1993). Sound pastoral advice on four aspects of devotional space in churches; important background reading for anyone involved with renovation of a church building.

DeSanctis, Michael E., *Meeting House Essays: Renewing the City of God* (Chicago: Liturgy Training Publications, 1994). A new overview of the reform of Catholic church architecture in the United States since 1962. DeSanctis examines its theological foundations in the conciliar and postconciliar documents, its roots in European design and its significance for the church of the next century.

Bishops' Committee on the Liturgy, *Environment and Art in Catholic Worship.* A fundamental document not only for matters of art and architecture but for understanding the basic importance of the assembly. Available in *The Liturgy Documents.*

Fischer, Balthasar, *Signs, Words and Gestures* (Collegeville: The Liturgical Press, 1981). Simple homilies containing important but often neglected information. Written by one of the authors of Vatican II's reform of the liturgy.

Mauck, Marchita, *Shaping a House for the Church* (Chicago: Liturgy Training Publications, 1990). A short book that details various aspects and components of the liturgical environment.

Bishops' Committee on the Liturgy, *Music in Catholic Worship* and *Liturgical Music Today.* The 1972 statement *Music in Catholic Worship* is the foundation for pastoral music while the 1982 document *Liturgical Music Today* spells out further implications for the role of music and musicians. Available in *The Liturgy Documents.*

Resources for *Who Does the Liturgy?*

Bishops' Committee on Priestly Life and Ministry, *Fulfilled in Your Hearing: The Homily in the Sunday Assembly.* A brief and very helpful description of the role and preparation of the homily. Available in *The Liturgy Documents.*

Hovda, Robert, *Strong, Loving and Wise,* (Collegeville: The Liturgical Press, 1977). The principles and practice of presiding: the presider's spirit, role in planning, preparation, presence, style.

Mazar, Peter, *To Crown the Year* (Chicago: Liturgy Training Publications, 1995). A book that walks through the church year making valuable suggestions about how to enhance the environment to help the assembly pray the liturgy.

Rosser, Aelred, *A Well-Trained Tongue: Formation in the Ministry of Reader* (Chicago: Liturgy Training Publications, 1983). The role and spirit of the lector: brief discussions and extended exercises for beginning and advanced lectors.

Ryan, G. Thomas, *The Sacristy Manual* (Chicago: Liturgy Training Publications, 1993). A unique book for all those who care for the church building in view of helping to celebrate the liturgy well. Chock full of information and helpful suggestions.

Resources for *The Mass*

Bernardin, Cardinal Joseph, *Guide for the Assembly* (Chicago: Liturgy Training Publications, 1997). Pastoral letter on parish Sunday eucharist and the responsibility of the assembly.

Huck, Gabe, *The Communion Rite at Sunday Mass* (Chicago: Liturgy Training Publications, 1989). A thorough and engaging discussion of the Sunday communion rite, with background and practical hints. Useful for planners, ministers, catechists and all who love the liturgy.

Huck, Gabe, *Preaching about the Mass* (Chicago: Liturgy Training Publications, 1992). A collection of sample homilies and reprintable bulletin inserts whose purpose is to help the assembly better appreciate various parts and aspects of the Mass.

Lectionary for Mass: Introduction. The 1982 revision of the introduction to the lectionary is a concise but thorough understanding of the order and ministries involved in the liturgy of the word as well as the role and structure of the lectionary. Available in *The Liturgy Documents.*

Searle, Mark, *Liturgy Made Simple* (Collegeville: The Liturgical Press, 1981). An outstanding introduction to the structure and celebration of Sunday Mass.

Seasoltz, Kevin, ed., *Living Bread, Saving Cup: Readings on the Eucharist* (Collegeville: The Liturgical Press, 1982) Articles previously published in *Worship* on a variety of questions related to the eucharist.

Resources for *Days and Seasons*

Adam, Adolf, *The Liturgical Year* (Collegeville: The Liturgical Press, 1992). A survey of the history and current reform of the feasts and seasons.

Huck, Gabe, *The Three Days*, rev. ed. (Chicago: Liturgy Training Publications, 1992). The planning and celebration of the liturgies of Holy Thursday, Good Friday and the Easter Vigil.

Nocent, Adrian, *The Liturgical Year* (Collegeville: The Liturgical Press, 1977). Four volumes with detailed notes on the seasons and feasts, their history, theology and celebration.

Schmemann, Alexander, *Great Lent* (Crestwood NY: St. Vladimir's Seminary Press, 1969). An Orthodox theologian, Schmemann conveys the strength and beauty of the lenten season.

Resources for *The Rites of the Church*

Catholic Household Blessing and Prayers (Washington: USCC, 1988) The official U.S. resource book for common prayers, daily blessings, days and seasons, and for the blessing of family members in various times and places.

Fitzgerald, Timothy, *Confirmation: A Parish Celebration* (Chicago: Liturgy Training Publications, 1998). Detailed examination of the rite of confirmation for planners and ministers.

Gusmer, Charles, *And You Visited Me: Pastoral Care of the Sick* (Collegeville: The Liturgical Press, 1992). Development of the rites of the sick and a guide to their pastoral implementation in the parish.

Kavanagh, Aidan, *The Shape of Baptism: The Rite of Christian Initiation* (Collegeville: The Liturgical Press, 1992). Outstanding study of the church's initiatory practices and implications of the Rite of Christian Initiation of Adults.

Lewinski, Ronald, *Welcoming the New Catholic*, rev. ed. (Chicago: Liturgy Training Publications, 1994). The introduction and use of the *Rite of Christian Initiation of Adults* in the parish.

Martos, Joseph, *Doors to the Sacred* (Ligouri: Ligouri Press, 1991). History of the rites through the present.

Rutherford, Richard, *The Death of a Christian: The Rite of Funerals* (Collegeville: The Liturgical Press, 1991). The history, theology and celebration of the reformed rites for the burial of the dead.

Schmemann, Alexander, *Of Water and the Spirit* (Crestwood NY: St. Vladimir's Seminary Press, 1974). A study of initiation in the Orthodox tradition which offers many insights for those of other rites.

Searle, Mark, *Christening: The Making of Christians* (Collegeville: The Liturgical Press, 1982). History and detailed study of the ritual for infant baptism and confirmation.

Simons, Thomas, *Blessings for God's People,* rev. ed. (Notre Dame: Ave Maria Press, 1995). Daily, annual and occasional blessings gathered from many sources.

The Rites (Collegeville: The Liturgical Press, 1984; 2nd ed., 1992). Complete introductions and rites for adult initiation, infant baptism, confirmation, penance, marriage, pastoral care of the sick and funerals.

Sources

Page iv, from *Environment and Art in Catholic Worship,* # 9. Copyright © 1978 United States Catholic Conference, Inc. (USCC). Used with permission. All rights reserved.

Page 3, Romano Guardini, from *The Spirit of the Liturgy.* Translated by Ada Lane. New York: Sheed and Ward, 1935. German publication: 1918. Reprinted by permission of Sheed and Ward, an Apostolate of the Priests of the Sacred Heart. 7373 South Lovers Land Road, Franklin, Wisconsin 53132.

Page 3, Evelyn Underhill, from *Worship.* New York: Harper & Row, 1936.

Page 5, Aidan Kavanaugh, from *Elements of Rite: A Handbook of Liturgical Style.* New York: Pueblo, 1982, page 103.

Page 5, Evelyn Underhill, from *Worship.* New York: Harper & Row, 1936.

Page 7, Nathan Mitchell, from "Amen Corner," in *Worship* (March 1992).

Page 7, Jane Gaden, from *Communion in Australian Churches,* Joint Board of Christian Education in Melbourne.

Page 9, Robert W. Hovda, from *Dry Bones: Living Worship Guide to Good Liturgy.* Washington: The Liturgical Conference, 1973, pages 80–81. Copyright © 1973 The Liturgical Conference, 8750 Georgia Ave., Suite 123, Silver Spring, MD 20910-3621. All rights reserved. Used with permission.

Page 9, Virginia Sloyan, from *Liturgy: Covenant with the World.* Copyright © The Liturgical Conference, 8750 Georgia Ave., Suite 123, Silver Spring, MD 20910-3621. All rights reserved. Used with permission.

Page 13, Aelred Rosser, from *A Well-Trained Tongue.* Chicago: Liturgy Training Publications, 1996, page 3.

Page 13, Karl Rahner, from *The Eternal Year.* Baltimore: Helicon Press, 1964.

Page 15, Mark Searle, from *Christening: The Making of Christians.* Collegeville: The Liturgical Press, 1980, page 51.

Page 15, from *Fulfilled in Your Hearing,* #35, Copyright © 1982 USCC. Used with permission. All rights reserved.

Page 17, Romano Guardini, from *Sacred Signs.* St. Louis: Pio Decimo Press, 1956, page 18.

Page 19, Janet Schlichting, "Processing," in *Assembly* (December 1979).

Page 19, Gordon Lathrop, from *Holy Things: A Liturgical Theology.* Minneapolis: Fortress Press, 1993, page 121.

Page 21, Romano Guardini, from *Sacred Signs.* St. Louis: Pio Decimo Press, 1956, pages 13–14.

Page 23, Godfrey Diekmann, from *Pastoral Music in Practice.* Washington: Pastoral Press, 1990.

Page 23, John Wesley, from *United Methodist Hymnal.* Nashville: The United Methodist Publishing House, 1989, page vii.

Page 25, Nathan Mitchell, from "A God Who Hears," in *Pastoral Music in Practice.* Washington: Pastoral Press, 1990, pages 58–59.

Page 25, Alice Parker, from *Melodious Accord: Good Singing in Church.* Chicago: Liturgy Training Publications, 1991.

Page 25, from *Constitution on the Sacred Liturgy,* #114. In *Documents on the Liturgy.* Collegeville: Liturgical Press, 1982, page 24. Excerpts from the English translation of *Documents on the Liturgy, 1963–1979: Conciliar, Papal, and Curial Texts* copyright © 1982, International Commission on English in the Liturgy, Inc., (ICEL). All rights reserved.

Page 27, from *Liturgical Music Today* #47–48. Copyright © 1982 USCC. Used with permission. All rights reserved.

Page 29, Marty Haugen, "All Are Welcome," #753 in *Gather Comprehensive.* Chicago: GIA Publications, Inc., 1994. Copyright © 1994 by GIA Publications.

Page 31, from *Environment and Art in Catholic Worship,* #19–21. Copyright © 1978 USCC. Used with permission. All rights reserved.

Page 33, Psalm 84, from the English translation of the *Liturgical Psalter,* copyright © 1994 ICEL. All rights reserved.

Page 33, from *Environment and Art in Catholic Worship,* #4. Copyright © 1978 USCC. Used with permission. All rights reserved.

Page 35, from a Shaker hymn, "'Tis the gift to be simple," text from *The Hymnal 1982,* Church Pension Fund.

Page 37, Romano Guardini, from *The Spirit of the Liturgy.* Reprinted by permission of Sheed and Ward, an Apostolate of the Priests of the Sacred Heart. 7373 South Lovers Land Road, Franklin, Wisconsin 53132.

Page 39, Cardinal Roger Mahony, from *Gather Faithfully Together: Guide for Sunday Mass*. Chicago: Liturgy Training Publications, 1997, page 10.

Page 43, from *Constitution on the Sacred Liturgy*, #7. *In Documents on the Liturgy*. Collegeville: Liturgical Press, 1982. Excerpts from the English translation of *Documents on the Liturgy, 1963–1979: Conciliar, Papal, and Curial Texts* copyright © 1982, ICEL. All rights reserved.

Page 43, Mary Collins.

Page 45, from *Environment and Art in Catholic Worship*, #28–29. Copyright © 1978 USCC. Used with permission. All rights reserved.

Page 45, Cardinal Joseph Bernardin, from *Guide for the Assembly*. Chicago: Liturgy Training Publications, 1997, page 5.

Page 47, Robert Hovda, from *Strong, Loving and Wise*. Washington: The Liturgical Conference, 1977, pages 10–11. Copyright © 1977 The Liturgical Conference, 8750 Georgia Ave., Suite 123, Silver Spring, MD 20910-3621. All rights reserved. Used with permission.

Page 49, Austin Fleming, from *Preparing for Liturgy*. Chicago: Liturgy Training Publications, 1997, page 117.

Page 51, Cardinal Richard Cushing, from his pastoral letter *Liturgy and Life*. Boston: Daughters of St. Paul, 1964.

Page 51, Cardinal Joseph Bernardin, from *Guide for the Assembly*. Chicago: Liturgy Training Publications, 1997, page 14.

Page 53, Robert Lowry, from "How Can I Keep from Singing," adapted with additional lyrics by Doris Plenn, copyright © 1957 (renewed) by Sanga Music, Inc. All rights reserved.

Page 55, Aelred Rosser, from *A Well-Trained Tongue*. Chicago: Liturgy Training Publications, 1996, page 1.

Page 57, David Philippart, from *Serve God With Gladness: A Manual for Servers*. Chicago: Liturgy Training Publications, 1998, page 8.

Page 59, David Philippart, from *Saving Signs, Wondrous Words*. Chicago: Liturgy Training Publications, 1996, page 20.

Page 61, Austin Fleming, from *Preparing for Liturgy*. Chicago: Liturgy Training Publications, 1997, page 106.

Page 63, Flannery O'Connor, from "Letter to 'A,' July 20, 1955," in *Habit of Being*. New York: Vintage Books, 1979, page 90.

Page 63, Frederick R. McManus, from *Sacramental Liturgy*. New York: Herder & Herder, 1967.

Page 65, G. Thomas Ryan, from *The Sacristy Manual*. Chicago: Liturgy Training Publications, 1993, page 18.

Page 65, Pope Paul VI, from his address to the Italian national congress of diocesan and liturgical commissions on liturgy and sacred art, January 4, 1967, in *Documents on the Liturgy*. Collegeville: The Liturgical Press, 1982, page 1356. Excerpts from the English translation of *Documents on the Liturgy, 1963–1979: Conciliar, Papal, and Curial Texts* copyright © 1982, ICEL. All rights reserved.

Page 67, Thomas O. Simons and James M. Fitzpatrick, from *The Ministry of Liturgical Environment*. Collegeville: The Liturgical Press, 1984, page 15.

Page 67, Austin Fleming, from *Preparing for Liturgy*. Chicago: Liturgy Training Publications, 1997, page 130.

Page 67, Cecilia Davis Cunningham, from *Art, Creativity and the Sacred*. Diane Apostolos, ed. New York: Crossroad, 1984.

Page 71, Mark Searle, from *Sunday Morning: A Time for Worship*. Collegeville: The Liturgical Press, 1982, page 8.

Page 71, Mark Searle, from "Keeping Sunday," in *Assembly* (June 1981).

Page 73, Cardinal Joseph Bernardin, from *Guide for the Assembly*. Chicago: Liturgy Training Publications, 1997, page 20.

Page 73, Gerard S. Sloyan, from *Worshipful Preaching*. Minneapolis: Fortress Press, 1984.

Page 75, Walter J. Burghardt, SJ, from *Preaching the Just Word*. New Haven: Yale University Press, 1996, page 1.

Page 77, Abraham Joshua Heschel, from *Man's Quest for God*. New York: Simon and Schuster, 1954.

Page 79, Huub Oosterhuis, from *Zomaar een dak boven wat hoofen*, "What is this Place?" translated by David Smith. Text and arrangement © 1967, Gooi en Sticht, bv., Baarn, The Netherlands. All rights reserved. Exclusive agent for English-language countries: OCP Publications, 5536 NE Hassalo, Portland OR 97213. All rights reserved. Used with permission.

Page 81, Pierre Teilhard de Chardin, from *The Divine Milieu*. New York: Harper and Row, 1957, 1960.

Page 83, Nathan D. Mitchell and John K. Leonard, from *The Postures of the Assembly during the Eucharistic Prayer*. Chicago: Liturgy Training Publications, 1994, pages 78–79.

Page 85, Walter Burghardt, SJ, from *Love is a Flame of the Lord: More Homilies on the Just Word*. New York: Paulist Press, 1995, page 73.

Page 85, Bishop Donald Trautman, from "Maranatha: Centrality of the Eucharist," in *Origins*, vol. 23 (January 13, 1994).

Page 87, Saint Augustine, *Sermo* 272 as translated in Daniel Sheerin, *The Eucharist*. Wilmington, DE: Michael Glazier, 1986.

Page 87, Christina Neff, Saint Nicholas Church, Evanston, Illinois.

Page 89, William R. Crockett, from *Eucharist: Symbol of Transformation*. New York: Pueblo, 1989, page 256.

Page 89, Abraham Joshua Heschel, from *Man's Quest for God*. New York: Simon and Schuster, 1954.

Page 93, from *General Norms for the Liturgical Year and Calendar*, #1. In *Documents on the Liturgy*. Collegeville: Liturgical Press, 1982, page 1155. Excerpts from the English translation of *Documents on the Liturgy, 1963–1979: Conciliar, Papal, and Curial Texts* copyright © 1982, ICEL. All rights reserved.

Page 95, W. H. Auden, from "For the Time Being: A Christmas Oratorio," from *W.H. Auden: Collected Poems* by W. H. Auden, edited by Edward Mendelson. Copyright © 1944 and renewed 1972 by W. H. Auden. Reprinted by permission of Random House, Inc.

Page 95, Cardinal John Henry Newman.

Page 97, Dietrich Bonhoeffer, from "December 17, 1943," in *Letters and Papers from Prison*. London: SCM Press, 1953, 1967, 1971.

Page 97, Nathan Mitchell, from *Liturgy*, vol. 1 no. 2. Washington: The Liturgical Conference, 1980. Copyright © 1980 The Liturgical Conference, 8750 Georgia Ave., Suite 123, Silver Spring, MD 20910-3621. All rights reserved. Used with permission.

Page 99, Peter Mazar, from *Lent Sourcebook*, volume 1. Chicago: Liturgy Training Publications, 1990, page vi.

Page 101, Karl Rahner, from *The Great Church Year: The Best of Karl Rahner's Homilies, Sermons, and Meditations*. New York: Crossroad, 1993, page 192.

Page 101, Dietrich Bonhoeffer, from *I Loved This People*. Atlanta: John Knox Press, 1965.

Page 103, from *Economic Justice for All*, #47. Copyright © 1986 USCC. Used with permission. All rights reserved.

Page 103, Abbot Patrick Regan from "The Fifty Days and the Fiftieth Day," in *Worship* (May, 1981) pages 197–198.

Page 105, Mary Ellen Hynes, from *Companion to the Calendar*. Chicago: Liturgy Training Publications, 1993, page 23.

Page 109, Abraham Joshua Heschel, from *Man's Quest for God*. New York: Simon and Schuster, 1954, page 32.

Page 109, Flannery O'Connor, from "Letter to Janet McKane, May 17, 1963," in *The Habit of Being*. New York: Vintage Books, 1979, page 521.

Page 111, from an inscription in the baptistry of St. John Lateran, Rome; translated by Aidan Kavanagh in *The Shape of Baptism*. New York: Pueblo, 1978, page 49.

Page 113, Alex Haley, from *Roots*. Copyright © 1976 by Alex Haley. Used by permission of Doubleday, a division of Bantam Doubleday Dell Publishing Group, Inc.

Page 115, Balthasar Fisher, from *Signs, Words and Gestures*. Collegeville: The Liturgical Press, 1981.

Page 117, Sherril Jaffe, from "Abraham Tells Ann He Loves Her," in *The Unexamined Wife*. Santa Barbara: Black Sparrow Press, 1983.

Page 117, Regis Duffy, from *Real Presence: Worship, Sacraments, and Commitment*. New York: Harper and Row, 1982, page 2.

Page 119, from the *Pastoral Constitution on the Church in the Modern World*, #30. Excerpts from *Vatican Council II: The Conciliar and Post Conciliar Documents, New Revised Edition* edited by Austin Flannery, OP, copyright © 1992, Costello Publishing Company, Inc., Northport, NY are used by permission of the publisher, all rights reserved. No part of these excerpts may be reproduced, stored in a retrieval system, or transmitted in any form or by any means — electronic, mechanical, photo-copying, recording or otherwise — without express permission of Costello Publishing Company.

Page 121, Flannery O'Connor, from "Letter to 'A,' June 28, 1956," in *Habit of Being*. New York: Vintage Books, 1979, page 163.

Page 121, Willa Cather, from "Old Mrs. Harris," in *Collected Stories*. New York: Vintage Classics, 1992, page 270.

Page 123, from *General Introduction to the Order of Christian Funerals*, #6, © 1985 ICEL. All rights reserved.